Creating Community

Creating Community

The Art of Empowerment in Community Association Living

MICHAEL ROBERT PIERSON

authorHOUSE®

AuthorHouse™
1663 Liberty Drive
Bloomington, IN 47403
www.authorhouse.com
Phone: 1-800-839-8640

First published by AuthorHouse   08/22/2011

ISBN: 978-1-4567-9588-7 (sc)
ISBN: 978-1-4567-9587-0 (hc)
ISBN: 978-1-4567-9586-3 (ebk)

Library of Congress Control Number: 2011915106

Printed in the United States of America

Any people depicted in stock imagery provided by Thinkstock are models, and such images are being used for illustrative purposes only.
Certain stock imagery © Thinkstock.

This book is printed on acid-free paper.

CONTENTS

INTRODUCTION 1

LEARNING TO LET GO IN ORDER TO
    BRING PEOPLE TOGETHER 9

WHAT COMMUNITY LOOKS LIKE............................. 20

COMMUNICATION TOOLS 64

COMMITTEE WORK.. 102

COMPASSIONATE INVOLVEMENT 133

ESCAPING THE HIJACKERS...................................... 141

LEADERSHIP 159

IT'S A COMMUNITY.. 184

CONCLUSION.. 201

REFERENCES 204

ACKNOWLEDGMENTS 209

INTRODUCTION

Creating Community

*"Man did not weave the web of life—he is merely a strand in it.
Whatever he does to the web, he does to himself."*

Chief Seattle, 1854

There is an ancient wisdom tale that I share with groups whenever I have the opportunity to speak to them that sums up the mission of this book:

A very wise old teacher was walking with his pupil when the student asked him, "Teacher, what is the difference between heaven and hell?" The teacher took his pupil's hand and replied, "Let me show you." And with that they were transported into a huge banquet room with tables laden with the most delicious foods known to man. At the tables sat countless men and women, however, instead of hands and arms, they each had a fork and spoon attached to their shoulders that were so long that they were unable to get any of the feast laid out in front of them into their mouths. Moans and groans of agony and frustration filled the air. "What is this, teacher?" asked the pupil. "This, my son, is hell," replied the teacher.

In an instant, they were transported into another banquet room with exactly the same delicious food laid upon endless tables and there were countless men and women sitting at the tables with the same forks and spoons attached to their shoulders. However, instead of moans and groans of frustration there was laughter and song and the air was filled with the sounds of happiness. "What is this, teacher?" the pupil asked once again. "This, my son, is heaven." The teacher responded. "But, teacher, this is exactly like the other room we were in. Are heaven and hell the same?" inquired the puzzled student. "No. Not at all," said the teacher. "In the first room the people were in anguish because they could not get any of the sumptuous food into their mouths. But, here in heaven, there is incredible joy and everyone is enjoying unlimited abundance because instead of being unable to feed themselves, they are feeding each other."

Why does that story touch me so deeply? Because it illustrates the difference between "me" thinking and "we" thinking. The gap between those two ways of thought is what this book will attempt to shrink. Like the occupants in heaven feeding each other, each of us can learn ways to embrace community-consciousness and, metaphorically, feed and empower the people and environment around us. When people think solely of themselves, or their family unit, or their company, and are blind to fact that their "me" life can be GREATLY enhanced by embracing their "we" life, then community cannot be created. Community remains just a shallow, meaningless word and both their "me" and their "we" lives suffer.

The Merriam-Webster Dictionary defines "Community" as "a unified body of individuals." To be unified is to unite and bring people together. Community association living is one of the greatest modern experiments of bringing people together in a residential environment outside of the creation of organized cities. However, if it were as simple as bringing people together to make them unified, then there would be no reason to write this book. As anyone who has ever lived within or worked around community associations knows, bringing people together physically—as in a community association—often creates the opposite condition to unity: division, discord, dispute, apathy and conflict. Each of those attitudes and behaviors contribute to community associations that are difficult to live in, have few volunteers to serve on the board or committees, suffer from apathy—no one attends board meetings, or votes at annual meetings, and there is a challenge with compliance to rules and regulations—are extremely challenging to manage and difficult to work with. If any of these conditions seem familiar, I urge you to read on.

The goal of this book is to help those people whose lives are impacted by community association living—owners, residents, board members, volunteers, management staff and the business partners that service them—have a clearer understanding of the dynamics about how to create a community in the truest sense of the word: A collection of diverse individuals that are engaged with each other, informed about community issues, and actively work together in order to accomplish goals that will make the community stronger and each of their individual lives better. In short, it is about the art of empowerment in community association living.

No one has ever accomplished much, either as an individual or as a group, if they did not feel as if they mattered, if they did not feel as if they had some degree of control over their life. It is that "victim" mentality that begins the frustrating cycle of division, discord, dispute, apathy and conflict that far too many community associations suffer from. If you act like a victim, you are more likely to be treated as one and the vicious cycle will continue indefinitely unless there is change. My hope is that this book will promote and encourage that change: the change from a sense of powerlessness and victimization to a sense of empowerment and control, at the individual and at the group level.

I want to ask at the beginning of our time together, for you (the reader) to suspend any pessimism you may hold regarding creating community due to past experiences, failures or awareness of the difficulty of encouraging a collection of uninterested people to buy-into the concepts presented in this book. There is no doubt that creating community consciousness is an extremely difficult task given the many obstacles that we face. Those obstacles come in the form of individual, group and cultural dynamics that promote selfishness instead of selflessness. Beginning a successful journey to creating community demands an open mind and willingness to risk change. It demands a change in your attitude about community. In a sense, you are going to have to leave community in order to achieve community. What I mean by that is that you must leave your notion, your concept, and any failed experience of community behind in order to embrace a new way of thinking about the community that awaits you. I have to assume that if you are reading this book that your experience of community is not as wonderful as you think it could be. However, if you didn't think a sense of community was possible, then I doubt you would be choosing to spend your valuable time with this book. I invite you to hold close to you those thoughts that believe true community is possible. It is that embrace that will comfort you on this journey and will invite others to join you. Everything you do is guided by thought. The world you inhabit and see is shaped by the way you see it. The way you see is shaped by the way you think. So, if you really want to change your life, or your community, the best way to change it is to change the way you think. I want to help you change the way you think about creating community.

The mystery of creating community is very intriguing. Everything we know about community, about life in general, is contained within the terminology of the concept of opposites. We always think in terms of opposites (good/bad; black/white; right/wrong), but the experience of true community is beyond the pair of opposites. It is the experience of unity and unity embraces all, it transcends all. As ambitious as it may sound, by the end of this book it is my hope that the reader will learn a new way of relating to, connecting with, and experiencing those people they share their life with and around.

I will illustrate strategies that owners and residents can use to help them redefine their perceptions of themselves, their community and their place within their community. I want to share simple, yet profound, management strategies that board members, volunteers and management can utilize to attract the energy of change needed in order to bring people together towards the pursuit of common goals and objectives. I also aim to help educate community business partners (those people that serve community associations, whether it is maintaining their landscaping or selling them common area insurance) about the dynamics at play within every community association in order to join them in their quest for community and increase the perceived value of their service and their business.

Even though this book is aimed at those people who have a role in community associations, I encourage you to apply many of these strategies and techniques in other areas of your life in which you want to strengthen your relationships. Certain elements of creating community are accurate metaphors for many other life challenges. It will be up to you to decipher them. You could be a small business owner, an office manager, a sales representative, a law enforcement officer or a teacher, I guarantee that there is something here that can help you unite others and help create community consciousness within the scope of many of your other life roles.

In order to accomplish those goals, I will be sharing some of my own experiences living within community associations, managing community associations and working with dozens and dozens of associations, boards, committees, community association managers, and as the owner of a publishing company that specializes in community association communication tools. I will also be drawing heavily from my first book (Taking Control: Time Management and Communication Tools for Community Association Management) as it deals with one of the most important elements of creating community: communication.

I also want to share my feelings, at the beginning of our time together, about how very privileged I am to have worked with some incredibly talented and skilled community association and management professionals whose tutelage, guidance and support—in so many ways both personally and professionally throughout the years—have helped form the foundation of the community building philosophy I will share with you in these pages. The list is a long one and I can't include everyone, but I especially want to thank Thomas Peter von Bahr, Lou Barone, Steve Townsend, William & Desda Monaghan, Carol Whitlock, Marianne Simek, Steven Shuey, Julie Adamen, and most importantly, Jan Lhotka, who without her unique ability to bring out the best in everyone she comes in contact with, I would never be a position to write this book today.

Finally, I will be borrowing and reinforcing this thesis with poems, stories and the wisdom quotes of some of the world's greatest thinkers in order to show that the material I am presenting is not new, just redefined to fit our purposes. The reason for the poems, wisdom quotes, humor, etc., is that creating community is a subject that is traditionally a focus of left-brain thinking. Roger Sperry, a Nobel Prize winner, initiated the study of the relationship that exists between the brain's right and left hemispheres. Sperry found that the left half of the brain tends to function by processing information in an analytical, rational, logical, sequential way. The right half of the brain tends to function by recognizing relationships, integrating and synthesizing information, and arriving at intuitive insights.

In other words, the left side of your brain deals with a problem, or situation, by collecting data, making analyses and using rational thinking processes to reach a logical conclusion. The right side of your brain approaches the same problem or situation by making intuitive leaps to answers based on insights and perceptions. The left brain tends to break information apart for analysis, while the right brain tends to put information together to synthesize a whole picture.

Research into the brain's function and individuals' brain dominance was further enhanced by Ned Hermann, the former manager of management education at General Electric's Management Development Institute. Herman developed a brain-dominance profile instrument to help people assess the manner in which they use their brains. Hermann's research suggests that people in various professions tend to be either left-brain or right-brain oriented. Managers (board members & community association managers), for instance, tend to be left-brain dominant, focusing on organizing, structuring, and controlling situations. Social workers tend to be right-brain dominant, drawing on their ability to relate to emotions to achieve insights about situations. I believe the reason that creating community is so difficult for community association leaders is because the foundation of developing community-consciousness requires substantial right-brain thinking (creativity, flexibility, compassion, opportunity thinking) but it is usually dealt with using left-brain logic.

For left-brain thinkers, creating community is often a systematic and detailed hunt using known procedures methods and analysis, no matter how effective, because it is what they have been taught and has worked for them in the private business sector. For the left-brain thinker, everything is based upon objective perception and accountability. In many cases, this is exactly what an organization needs from a quality standpoint. For right-brain thinkers, however, creating community can be regarded as a tool for identifying opportunities for continuous improvement and growth using innovative and creative community-building efforts. Finding the balance to effect real change requires addressing both aspects of how we think. Poetry, humor, mental exercises that challenge what we value, and wisdom stories all are right-brain stimulators. Lists, descriptions, characteristics and facts are all left-brain stimulators.

Many of the other books and information that I have researched seem to focus primarily on left-brain stimulators and, I surmise, may contribute to the dismal success rate of helping people get along with each other (social work in its truest sense) and build a base of unity. If relying on left-brain activities worked on their own, creating community would not be such a complicated process. So, the poetry, quotes and stories may lose some of you because it may not fit into your paradigm of what you expect in dealing with the subject matter, but if given enough attention, they will open up one's perception by encouraging a broader sense of understanding and exercise your right-brain thinking effectiveness, a necessary requirement in creating community.

Like all change in life, creating community out of disunity may appear a bit daunting and it is easy for the fear of the unknown to keep us frozen in place. It's the old "devil we know" mindset. Change has it rewards, but it also has its costs. Initially, it is an investment of time and it is a process that is always ongoing and not without failures. The 'perfect' community association does not exist and there will always be work to do. Accepting imperfection is also an important step. As the songwriter/singer Leonard Cohen wrote, "There is a crack in everything, that's where the light gets in." However, that said, there is a logical progression of community growth that, if you risk following, will help you, your neighbors, your community and/or your company become a catalyst for creating strong, caring and vibrant community associations. It is a journey of awareness and a journey of allowing and, best of all, it is a journey of empowerment, growth, engagement and belonging . . . and it all begins with you!

LEARNING TO LET GO IN ORDER TO BRING PEOPLE TOGETHER

The Soul of Empowerment

"If you change one person, you change the world".
—The Talmud

You cannot change the problems of your community without first changing yourself. The first step on our journey to creating community is one that we have to take alone. It is the technique of learning how to let go. Pema Chodron, an American woman who was ordained as a Buddhist nun in the tradition of Tibetan Buddhism, writes in her book, "The Wisdom of No Escape" that letting go is the ability "to open beyond small-mindedness and to let go of any kind of fixation or limited view."

One of the greatest obstacles to creating community is our inability to put ourselves in other's shoes. To be unwilling to make the attempt to understand the perceptions and values of others and to believe that our view of the world and our community is the only correct one. That stance will destroy any and all efforts to create community because it feeds the urge to see what is wrong with the world instead of looking at what is right. Our viewpoint, our experiences and our skills are all important aspects of life that we need to use wisely if we are to achieve community-building success. However, it is our prejudices, our self-centeredness and our stubborness that will eventually sabotage everything that we are trying to achieve. We need to let go of those thoughts that are not reflective of certain core-values related to the community (community-consciousness). One of the attributes of a healthy community is that the residents abide with a sense of tranquility and calmness. That is only possible when the members of the community begin to see the positives in all situations and the character of the people around them.

You might be surprised to find that many of the problems that you perceive are not the same problems that others perceive. What you see as a problem may just be a reflection of your own issues with compliance, cooperation and/or belonging to something outside of your family unit or larger than yourself. I assure you that many community association problems are not self-inflicted, but in order to avoid wasting your time and energy, it is worth trying to discover which problems are worth pursuing and which are worth letting go of. For example, a resident's home (Let's call him Lou Sifer) is burglarized because he left their garage door open. Instead of taking responsibility for it by realizing it was the result of his failing to close the garage door (and comply with association rules), he blamed the security service (which regularly patrols the community streets) and the board of directors for failing to adequately protect the community. Lou's perception is based on an extremely selfish and limited view of the situation. Worse yet, if Lou were to be elected to the board of directors (motivated by his anger at the current board and backed by other owners who also look to blame the current board for any number of perceived bad decisions), then Lou can easily become a virus that infects any community-building process. If Lou were to take a step back, let go of his own story, view the situation more objectively and take responsibility, then a potential threat to creating community could have been avoided.

It is not only owners who incorrectly perceive situations and refuse to let go of their harmful perceptions. In 2006, the board president of a community association in Pagosa Springs, Colorado decided that he didn't like one of the other resident's holiday wreath shaped like a peace sign. He believed that it was offensive to the war effort in Iraq and Afghanistan, could be considered a symbol of Satan and because of its Pagan symbolism could be considered anti-Christ. Even though no other owners complained, he ordered the architectural control committee to tell the owner to remove the wreath. When the committee members refused, he fired them. If there was ever an example of someone hijacking their community in order to serve their own self-interests (the opposite of creating community), it was this guy. Ultimately, because of his actions, the owners of this association united (created community) and he and two other board members were forced to resign and a new board was elected that better represented the best interests of the owners. The association apologized to the owners with the peace sign wreath and they all lived happily ever after. I want to add that even though the community united because of the actions of a dictator (fairly common throughout the world these days), I do not recommend this as a course of action in creating community. In other words, don't allow a Lou Sifer to hijack your association as a means to achieve community-building.

Letting go begins with the technique of examining just how "stuck" we are in our own life and recognizing whether or not our perceptions and preferences are getting in the way of becoming "unstuck." We have to choose between holding on to what we know and makes us feel comfortable, and letting go and start exploring areas of ourself and our relationships with others that may not be so comfortable. Creating community begins with you, the individual, so you are equipped to help others follow the trail that you are breaking. We are all role models (even Lou!), whether we want to be or not. The challenge is to become the type of role model that inspires others to want to be a part of what you are building. More importantly, however, when we choose to let go of our own small-mindedness, we open ourselves up to community-consciousness and all of the actions we make within the community will begin to reflect a desire to serve others instead of our own self-interests.

The best part of learning how to let go is that you don't have to do anything. Letting go is about "not" doing. Not being self-centered, not being rude, not being angry, not getting carried away by a sense of our own self-importance. Letting go is a process that is similar to the process of creating a sculpture. By slowly chipping away at those parts of ourself that are getting in the way of becoming who we really need to be in order to be a catalyst for community-consciousness, we eventually become that person. Recognizing that ego is the fuel behind nearly all self-deceptive thinking is one of the most critical products of letting go. When ego is recognized it loses a little of its power over our choices and instead of acting out of desire to feed our ego, we begin to act out of a desire to do the right thing for everyone around us . . . in everything that we do.

When community-consciousness—the realization that everyone in the community shares certain community values—inspires enough people within a community or within those people that work with community associations, then empowerment is inevitable. When there is empowerment, there is community. Everything in this book is aimed at empowering individuals and communication is the most important source of personal power. If you believe in the premise that when there is empowerment then there is community, then everything that you read from this pont on will reinforce that and, if followed, will help create community.

Empowerment is based upon **three simple tasks:**

1. *Find out what people are thinking* and what they believe the problems are.
2. *Let them* design the solutions.
3. *Get out of the way* and let them put those solutions into practice.

Simple tasks, difficult implementation. There are countless obstacles and obstructions to achieving those three goals and the greatest of those challenges is beginning with finding out what people think and what they believe the problems are. We have to 'let go' of our own internal belief systems, perceptions, prejudices and experiences in order to truly listen. Once we accomplish that, once we get out of our own way, we begin the first step of empowerment and the first step in creating community. Without truly listening we cannot find out what other people are thinking, we do not learn anything. So, if you are willing, let's continue.

Self-knowledge is the first step in letting go. After all, if we don't know who we are, what we value and what our own personal belief systems, prejudices and preferences are, then we have nothing to hold on to and can not let go of anything. More importantly, although our goal is to unite others, the only way to achieve that is to first know ourself. As it says in the Tao Te Ching:

He who knows others is wise;
He who knows himself is enlightened."

Let's do a couple of exercises to help us get a glimpse of who we are:

EXERCISE #1—*If you find yourself uncomfortable with this exercise, it might be because you really don't know what your belief systems are,* *what your values, prejudices or preferences are. Most of us create these personality elements unconsciously (unless you are Rush Limbaugh) and the only time you may be asked about them is when you are in therapy, using online dating services, or are a member of Facebook. Answer the following sentences:*

What are the things you love most about your life?

What are the things that you wish you could change about your life?

What do you think is right in the world today?

What do you think is wrong in the world today?

What makes you angry?

What are your best qualities?

If you were a tree, what kind of tree would you be? (Just kidding!)

Since I am not a therapist and this is only a book and I can't see your list, I am not going to try to interpret your answers. I leave that up to you. The purpose of this exercise is to help you "see" yourself. This process of "seeing" is where self-knowledge begins. What you have in front of you is a reflection of your perceptions, values, beliefs, prejudices and preferences. Were you surprised at any of your answers? If you show your list to your husband/wife and closest friends, would they recognize you by your answers?

EXERCISE #2—*List the qualities/values of someone that you would consider a leader, someone whose direction you would follow.*

If you compare your answers to exercise #1 to the list you just created, can you see yourself as a leader? Do your answers to exercise #1 reflect the attitude that you expect of a leader?

EXERCISE #3—By comparing the answers to the first two exercises, list the qualities and ways of thinking that you may need to let go of in order for you to consider yourself a leader.

Using the answers to exercise #3, you now have a tangible list of thought patterns, values, prejudices, preferences and perceptions that you may want to let go of in order to help put yourself in a position as an advocate of community-consciousness.

One of the world's greatest proponents of creating community was Confucius. For centuries in ancient China the people practiced a combination of Confucianism and Taoism. Taoism is concerned with creating harmony within the individual. Confucianism deals with creating harmony within the community. Confucius taught that you do not have to be a leader to play an honorable role and have a positive influence on your world. However, cultivating the qualities of a leader will ultimately put you in a position of leadership because the people around you will see that your actions reflect a desire to achieve the common good of all. People will cooperate with the virtuous. Whenever anyone does something for the benefit of others, perceptions have the opporutnity to change. It is important that the people around you perceive you as being moral and trustworthy. Working successfully with other people demands that you earn their trust and faith in your abilities and intentions by doing and being your best. Drop any agenda you may have and people will trust you more. When problems arise, they have the opportunity to be resolved because everyone is working together in unity, in harmony. When that happens, community is being created . . . but it all begins with you.

Roles: We can take the first three exercises a step further in order to help us further define those qualities that we need to let go of in order to facilitate community-consciousness by identifying the various roles we take on in our life. Throughout our life, those roles change. As a young man I was a son, student, employee. When I got married I became a husband, father, employer. As our journey through life progresses we add and drop roles as necessity demands. However, each role we take on has its own set of values and qualities that are needed in order to succeed in that role. Certainly there are core values that are shared within every role (i.e., honesty, sincerity, determination, etc.), but how I act as a husband does not necessarily translate into how I act as an employer. After all, I sleep with my wife and I don't sleep with my employees (my wife appreciates that!). I treat my children different than I treat my golfing buddies (My children are granted endless mulligans through life. My golfing buddies only get one per side). The qualities that I need to express in order to succeed in my life's roles are often specific to the role iteself. Let's examine this further:

EXERCISE #4—Get out a piece of paper and a pen and write down all of the roles that you have in your life in the order of their importance (i.e. #1: Wife; #2: Mother, etc.).

If you look at your list, you have a snapshot of your life as it exists right now. Basically it is a list of those things in your life that you value the most. Now, let's take this a step further:

EXERCISE #5—For each role, answer the following question:

What are the qualities that you feel are necessary in order to be successful in this role?

When you have completed exercise #5, you now have a set of directions—a map—to follow in order to succeed in each of the roles of your life. If in order to succeed as a husband, I feel that I need to be loving, kind, loyal, generous, non-judgemental and patient, then I know that those qualities are the things that I need to be aware of and cultivate in my marriage. Similarly, if I want to succeed as an employer, I need to be goal-oriented, thoughtful, patient, instructive and encouraging. Those are the qualities that I must embrace to be a successful employer.

Now, even though this is a book about community associations and the odds that you—the reader—are somehow connected with at least one community association, I'd be willing to bet that the one role that most of you missed was the one that is related to being either a member, affilliate or vendor of a community association. Why would that be? Probably because your affiliation with a community association is something that you choose not to be overly conscious of. Creating community demands that this perception change. Being affiliated with a community association certainly should not be in the top five roles in your life, but it should fit somewhere in the top ten, don't you think? After all, the investment you have in your home, your job, your business is a pretty important part of your life.

I have found that a majority of owners have an indifferent attitude about their community association role at best. At worst, some have a negative perception of their association and those people leading it. Management company staff, although their jobs revolve around community associations, often view their clients in the same light as a firewalker views the coals they have to walk across in order to get to the other side. Vendors frequently perceive their community association clients as complicated and hard to satisfy (sort of how I perceive my wife!). This indifferent/negative perception issue, ladies and gentlemen, is the FUNDAMENTAL reason why community associations suffer from apathy, non-compliance, rumor mongering and just plain unneighborly conduct. In short, it is the reason why there is no unity in the community!

No one ever involved themselves in anything that they really didn't care about. For many, their community association is thought of as an entity that either tells them what to do and not to do and/or takes their money. When someone has those kind of thought patterns it becomes extremely difficult to get them to contribute, cooperate and comply with anything associated with their community association. If you have dozens or even hundreds of people harboring those indifferent/ negative attitudes, then you have a snowball's chance in hell of creating community . . . and Lou Sifer will be your board president!

All of those attitudes have to change if you want to have any chance of creating community. How do we do that? The key is communication (remember, communication is the most important aspect of personal power and personal power/empowerment is what creates community). First, however, we have to continue the lonely and introspective work on ourselves because we can't give anything to others (such as community-consciousness) until we have it ourselves. We have to recognize that we do indeed have a role related to the community association we live in or work with and that we share certain community-related values with everyone else in the community. Then, we have to identify those qualities and values that are necessary in order to succeed in that role. If we remain aware of those positive qualities whenever we assume that role within the community association, then our perceptions will also begin to change positively and others will also begin to appreciate and embrace those qualities/values. When we change, we also change the world around us. As Leo Tolstoy, the acclaimed Russian writer noted, "Everyone thinks of changing the world, but no one thinks of changing himself." Awareness, patience and persistence is the key to personal and community change.

EXERCISE #6—*List the qualities that you feel are necessary to succeed in your role related to the community association(s) you live in or work with.*

This list contains all of the positive qualities and attitudes that you will need to build upon. It should become your mantra, of sorts. Something that you should look at frequently and reinforce through actions that reflect the qualities on the list. Don't worry, you will fail miserably at times, but as long as you keep at it and have a sincere resolve to continue with the work, you will become a beacon of community-consciousness.

We began this chapter talking about and identifying negative qualities/ attitudes that we need to let go of in order to help create community. Now, we have a list of qualities/attitudes that we need to embrace. We are still talking about letting go and this list of positive qualities represents the image of our finished sculpture, so to speak. Any thoughts, values, actions, attitudes, prejudices, or qualities that do not fit our sculpture must be let go of. Letting go is a life-long process. Surely, you've been learning to let go for most of your life. The difference between the kind of letting go you've probably experienced and the kind of letting go that I have been talking about is that life most likely forced your hand causing you to let go in order to avoid some kind of pain. In creating community you are learning how to let go in order to bring people together so that they can experience the fulfillment that comes from being engaged with others and being a part of something larger than themselves.

Now, let's examine what community looks like so that we can recognize the face of empowerment and know what it is we are trying to create . . .

WHAT COMMUNITY LOOKS LIKE

The Face of Empowerment

The more you include others, the more smoothly things flow and the more easily things come to you. When you give little or no help to others or put obstacles in their path, the universe—in the form of people and circumstances—gives little or no help to you because you have cut yourself off from the whole.

Eckhart Tolle, A New Earth

Now that we have taken the first step and have begun our own individual journey towards creating community, we need to define our ultimate goal so that we know where and what we are traveling towards. What are all the different but complimentary elements that make up a successful community association? How will we know when we have reached our destination? Better yet, will we ever truly reach it? This is the second step: Defining empowerment (which ultimately leads to community) so that we know which direction to go and how to get there.

Power vs Force

Ultimately, a successful community association is one that has flattened the hierarchy, reducing the distance between those served and those ruling. In order to accomplish that goal either less power has to be given to those leading or more power has to be given to those who are served. The power of the board of directors is set by governing documents and law, so unless we are prepared to take a legislative approach and change the law, we have to work towards increasing the power of those served. However, one factor exists that we need to be aware of because it impacts empowering those served. That factor is the relationship between power versus force.

In the community association dynamic, power is what the board of directors can legally do in pursuit of preserving, protecting and enhancing the common assets of the association. Force is the type of energy that is required in order to maintain power. One is based upon truth (power as defined by law) and the other is based upon manipulation (power as defined by the force required to maintain it). According to David R. Hawkins, M.D., Ph.D. author of Power vs Force—The Hidden Determinants of Human Behavior, here are some of the attributes of Power and Force:

- Force is associated with the partial, power with the whole
- Force must always be justified, power requires no justification
- Force always creates counter-force and its effect is limited by definition
- Force is a movement, power is a skill
- Force always moves against something, power doesn't move against anything at all
- Force is incomplete and therefore has to be fed energy constantly
- Power is total and complete in itself and requires nothing from outside
- Force constantly consumes while power energizes, supplies and supports
- Power gives life and energy, force takes these away
- Power is associated with compassion, force is associated with judgment
- Force requires proof and support, power is inarguable and not subject to proof (1)

Here is an example of how boards (or board members) misuse their power by the use of force from an association that I am familiar with that we will call Shady Dealings HOA:

The current board of directors of Shady Dealings is made up of a majority of owners who are also members of the golf club, a separate entity within the gated community. The governing documents give members of the golf club two (2) votes in any association-related elections (The original community was not gated and the extra vote was written into the CC&Rs as an incentive to golf club members—which consisted of many more members than there are today—to vote in favor of gating the community). There are 1800 owners and now roughly 350 golf club members. In order for a quorum to be achieved for most elections, 51% of members must submit their vote and/or proxy. The board uses the 1800 number to base their 51% on. So, 901 votes need to be cast in order to validate and hold any election. The golf club members want to maintain control of the association because they believe they have a more vested interest in the community (because they pay substantial golf club membership fees), so historically they get 100% of their members to vote, giving them 700 votes. That means that only 201 of the remaining 1450 owners need to vote in order to obtain a quorum.

There is a faction within Shady Dealings that wants to shift the balance of power back to the non-golf club member owners by electing non-golf club members to the board and repealing the two vote provision of the governing documents. Their reasoning is that just because golf club members have the money to join the golf club, doesn't mean that they deserve to have twice as many votes as any one else and impose their will on non-golf club members. In addition, people who don't even live in Shady Dealings, but are members of the golf club, also get two votes on any association-related election. Plainly, the situation is unfair and prejudiced . . . but it gets better . . .

The sitting board of Shady Dealings, in order to keep power, forces the management company to provide them with a list of owners that have voted weeks prior to the election. The board then makes sure that all of their golf club members are on that list and aggressively pursues other owners who are sympathetic to their cause (or risk not being invited to social events, parties and being shunned by other golf club members) to submit their ballots in order to ensure that, of the ballots submitted, they can guarantee, come election day, that they have 901 votes in their pocket. When the couple of non-golf club member board members attempt to do the same thing, the management company does not cooperate with them (and why should they, the non-golf club board members are in a minority on the board and they want to keep the management contract for Shady Dealings. This translates into making sure the majority golf club board members get what they want, regardless of whether it is legal or not). Needless to say, all attempts to empower the real majority of owners in Shady Dealings (who just happen to be non-golf club members) are sabotaged by the force applied by the sitting board to manipulate every association-related vote. The golf club members have hijacked the association and refuse to set it free. There is a lot of division, rumors, anger and frustration within the community. However, there is not enough . . . yet . . . to warrant more non-golf club member owners to vote because most of the non-golf club owners don't really care (indifference = no action).

So, the first face of empowerment and of a successful community is one in which power is shared and force, of any kind, is kept to a minimum. It is the face of inclusiveness, not exclusiveness.

John Heider, in his book "The Tao of Leadership—Leadership Strategies for a New Age" writes:

"The leader who understands how process unfolds uses as little force as possible and runs the group without pressuring people. When force is used, conflict and argument follow. The group field degenerates. The climate is hostile, neither open nor nourishing. The wise teacher runs the group without fighting to have things a certain way. The leader's touch is light. The leader neither defends nor attacks. Remember that consequences, not selfishness, is both the means of teaching and the teaching itself. Group members will challenge the ego of one who leads egocentrically. But one who leads selflessly and harmoniously will grow and endure."

A Sense of Belonging

Alienation is one of the chief reasons that people do not care about issues pertaining to their community association—or any other groups that they may belong to. The sociologist, Devorah Kalekin-Fishman believes "the term alienation refers to objective conditions, to subjective feelings, and to orientations that discourage participation." In a sense, our culture promotes alienation by promoting material possessions over relationships. The result is that no matter what you own, you still don't feel "complete" and you avoid becoming a part of something in order to avoid having to deal with this sense of "incompleteness" in comparison to everyone else. It is an unconscious human predicament that can only be addressed by first realizing that it exists.

It was between the 18th and 19th centuries, with the advent of the Industrial Revolution, when our culture began to shift from a relationship-valued society towards a material-valued society. Nearly every aspect of our society was changed as industry growth prompted more economic growth than at any other time in our history. As we produced more, we made more money. As we made more money, we bought more things. In the past 100 years we have shifted from a culture that loved people and used things to a culture that loves things and uses people. Being a part of a group larger than oneself—which was one of the historical elements of survival—was no longer needed. Objectivity as a value started to become epidemic in our society because most people strove for what could be seen by others (clothes, car, home, job) and not what could be felt (satisfaction, contentment, compassion).

Happiness became dependent upon what one wanted, not on what one had. The result was that no matter how much one acquired, it was never enough to ensure happiness because there was always something else to want and even when you got something the wanting didn't end. You wanted more and you wanted to keep what you already had. Another vicious cycle that ultimately results in a sense of alienation because what you are pursuing (happiness) can never be found in the things that our culture tells us should make us happy (material possessions). We internalize that frustration and unconsciously feel inferior to others (who we assume are happy), so we avoid belonging.

Some of the symptoms of alienation are unfriendliness, isolation and mistrust. Sound familiar? Of all the obstacles to creating community, the culturally reinforced sense of alienation may be the most difficult to overcome. The good news though, is that it can be! How? By creating something (community consciousness) that focuses more on the ideals of relationship than it does on the reality of desire. Tina Rosenberg, in her ground-breaking book, "Join The Club," terms such a success in overcoming disunity 'the social cure.' Rosenberg details many examples of how people's behavior can be changed, not through information or fear—which is our culture's historical approach—but by helping people get what they really care about most: the respect of their peers. A great example of that is Alcoholics Annonymous (AA). Alcoholics are by the very nature of their disease, selfish and alienated—usually from their family and friends—because of their drinking. However, regardless of expensive rehab facilities and new age redefinitions of alcoholism and treatment methods, the most successful form of treatment is attending AA meetings. The reason it works so well is that the person is given an opportunity to unite with others who share the value of controlling their desire for alcohol. They share their successes and their failures.

They have success at controlling that desire because they feel a part of something larger than themselves and realize that their life is better because of that participation and the relationships that are devevloped because of it. Alchololics Annonymous and 'The Social Cure' are based upon the power of peer pressure. The military has successfully use the peer pressure since wars began. As Tina Rosenberg points out:

Armies run on unit cohesion. For a young man with his life before him, leaving the relative safety of the foxhole to charge into enemy fire—often in the service of a cause he does not consider his own—is unnatural behavior. He does it for his buddies, and because his buddies' esteem reinforces his own identity as a brave soldier. Every good military commander exploits this phenomenon. Shakespeare's King Henry V uses it to rally hs troops to the Battle of Argincourt on Saint Crispin's Day in 1415. In the play, Henry's men are outnumbered five-to-one by the French. When his cousin, Westmoreland, wishes for ten thousand more men, Henry stills him with a speech ending in these words:

We few, we happy few, we band of brothers;
For he to-day that sheds his blood with me
Shall be my brother; be he ne'er so vile
This day shall gentle his condition:
And gentlemen in England now a-bed
Shall think themselves accurs'd they were not here,
And hold their manhoods cheap whiles any speaks
That fought with us upon Saint Crispin's day.

This is probably the most famous passage in all of Shakespeare's history plays, and it is an example of the social cure.

Reinforce positive peer relations among neighbors and apply it to community building efforts and we provide an opportunity for others to realize that their life is better by uniting with their neighbors and engaging in their association affairs. Most people will choose to overcome their sense of alienation and participate because they see the advantages of participating all around them through the engaged life of their neighbors. Ultimately, if you build it (community consciousness), they (the owners) will come.

One could argue that the desire to belong is in our genes. For tens of thousands of years, survival in the world was dependent upon the concept of strength in numbers. Someone going it alone really didn't have much of a chance of surviving. But if you had other humans around you, then you stood a better chance of not being something's lunch because you could protect each other. In addition, the more hunters there were, the more food there was. Community was created in order to survive. These days, as long as there is a MacDonald's and a Starbucks nearby, we do just fine. So, we have to find other ways to "feed" the members of our community. Later chapters will deal with the kinds of nourishment belonging to a community association can provide, but right now we just need to understand that, given the choice, belonging is innately more attractive to most people than being alone. Another great example of our deep desire to belong is the incredible popularity of web-based social networks, such as Facebook.

At the time of this writing, there are 500 million people around the world on Facebook with the average user having 130 friends. Technology is redefining what it means to "belong" faster than ever before. The bottom line is that people want to connect with each other. We seem to be undergoing a paradigm shift of massive proportions in directions that have never been possible before. Could it be that we are moving back towards a "loving people, using things" paradigm and away from the value of wanting more things because we think having those things will make us happy? I believe we are. I also believe that the time is ripe for empowerment and creating community-consciousness, not just within community associations but in all aspects of our life. People are becoming more open to having a conversation with the people around them because it helps them feel more connected to life. Our culture of consumerism is already taking advantage of that through the introduction of new smart phones, applications and programs that everyone "must" have in order to connect with others faster and more efficiently. However, the fact that people want to connect with others and belong to something larger than themselves is what is really important. As I said before, our culturally-induced sense of alienation may be the biggest obstacle to helping create community-consciousness, but change is in the air.

The psychotherapist and philosopher, Piero Ferrucci, writes: "The sense of belonging is a basic need and at the same time the answer to a question. We ask ourselves: What am I part of? And this question resembles—perhaps coincides with—another equally crucial question: Who am I? We belong to a family, a group, a society, a professional category; and the affiliations define us and give us reason for existing. Without this belonging, we would feel like nothing. It is hard, maybe impossible, to know who we are without some reference to others. That is why the sense of belonging is a basic need, like the need for food, water, or a roof over our heads."

Our sense of belonging can be rigid and rusty—and can be restricted to a tight circle. Or it can be free, flexible, and active even in the toughest situations, making life easier and more pleasing. It seems evident to me that these attitudes have to do with kindness. If I see you as different and I view you with suspicion, or at the best with cold neutrality, it is unlikely that I will feel kindly disposed toward you. If instead I look at you knowing we both belong to the human race, both have a similar nature, different experiences but the same roots and a common destiny, then it is probable I will feel openness, solidarity, empathy toward you. In other words, kindness.

And just as it is possible to modulate our own sense of belonging, so it is possible to influence that sense in others. We can make others feel included or excluded, and in different ways: by our words, our glances, our body language in general. Opportunities for helping others feel included come along regularly. We are all referees and players in this sport. We can cultivate our sense of belonging, and decide to include others or not. It is all a question of how kind we want to be.

The second face of empowerment is the face of belonging. It is providing an opportunity for others to join in, unite together and improve the quality of their lives.

Communication

Just as culturally-induced alienation may be our biggest obstacle on our journey towards empowerment and community, communication may be our most effective tool to use in order to reach our destination. Communication is an invitation to become engaged with others. Every conversation, whether it be physical, spoken or written, has the potential to empower. Every posture, gesture, dialogue, letter, newsletter, flyer, bulletin board, phone call, website or email has the potential to help create community. Through communication we inform, educate, motivate, direct, share and, most importantly, listen. It is through the listening aspect of communication that we begin to understand one another. With understanding comes the ability to find common ground with others and it is in that common ground that we can plant the seeds of unity.

Transparency: One of the most attractive components of communication when it comes to uniting people is its ability to achieve transparency in all community association affairs. Transparency is the full, accurate and timely disclosure of information. It is to be able to witness—through communication—what is being done and understand why. Without transparency there can be no trust built up between any entity involved in the community association. Without trust, no one is going to unite with you. The story of Shady Dealings HOA is the story of a community that is governed by a lack of transparency because the board is doing business behind everyone's back in order to get what "they" want and not what is in the best interests of the entire community. Chances people are willing to unite together and build a strong and successful community at Shady Dealings? Zilch.

Unless the board of directors of any community association promote a culture of transparency, there will never develop the level of trust and confidence in their efforts to create community. Everything that is done must be done, shared with all members equally and be in the best interests of the entire community. The exception, of course, is when the board meets in executive session. However, a board of directors cannot randomly just shoo away owners in order to conduct business behind their backs. Governing documents and state law usually define the purpose and scope of when a board can meet in executive session, which includes matters of litigation, contracts with non-owners, owner discipline—and the owner at issue is entitled to attend that portion of the meeting—and personnel matters. All other matters MUST be addressed in open session and owners should always be encouraged to attend. They may not be allowed to participate in the meeting, but they are usually permitted to attend and witness how and why the board makes the decisions that they do.

Even though some states require open meetings and set strict limits on the scope of executive sessions, do boards still meet in secret? Absolutely. Sometimes it is on purpose and sometimes it isn't. For example, it is not uncommon for a board to meet in executive session and as the environment is much looser than in open session with owners present, they can slip into discussions that should be held at open meetings. It is important that management remain aware of what is and is not appropriate for discussion at executive sessions and redirect the board when necessary. It is important for the board to always keep in the mind the purpose of executive session and obey the requirements if they want to embrace a culture of transparency and earn the trust of their owners.

It's not just board meetings that need to be open for owners to attend. All committee meetings also need to be held in open session. Not only does this reinforce the culture of transparency, but it also affords the opportunity for other owners to take an interest in a committee and decide to join . . . which is what creating community is all about.

What are some of the other things a board can do to promote a culture of transparency? Here are some other suggestions (some required by law!):

- Post upcoming meeting agendas on the community bulletin board or website at least four (4) days prior to the meeting
- Post previous meeting agendas on the community website
- Distribute previously approved board meeting minutes at meetings
- Post approved board meeting minutes on the community website
- Publish a newsletter on a regular basis that includes board meeting highlights, committee reports and information on upcoming maintenance projects
- Keep the community website up-to-date and relevant by including association documents, forms, meeting dates/times/ locations and management contact information

In the next chapter we will discuss the communication tools available (newsletters, websites and social networking) and their best uses in achieving transparency.

Another very important by-product of communication when creating community is its ability to inform, educate and encourage owners to participate in their community association.

Inform: Information is power and the more information you share with your owners or employees, the more power you share. When we share power we are treating others with deep respect because we are acknowledging that they are important. Whenever someone feels important, they are much more likely to continue or increase their involvement in that group. Some of the issues that you can inform owners on are:

- Maintenance Schedules
- Board meeting dates/time/location, agendas, minutes
- Upcoming community events (i.e., garage sales, social events, committee meetings, etc.)
- Important contact information
- Goals of the board of directors for the year

Educate: When we take the time to educate others, we are telling them that our future depends upon them. The owner of today is the board member of tomorrow. Education speaks directly to how much we value others. Again, like information, educating others is a sign of respect and importance. Some of the issues that you can educate owners on are:

- Community policies
- Explanation of issues that are regularly dealt with by the board (i.e., reserve study, financial reports, reporting procedures, legal disclosures, etc.)
- How board meetings are run
- How committees are run

Encourage: Communicating encouragement takes many forms when dealing with the community association dynamic. It can take the form of a verbal invitation, a written notice, a website update or an email. It's not difficult to realize the benefit of positive reinforcement in creating community. It is like honey to a bear, milk to a cat, a ham sandwich to a hobo . . . it feeds the community and helps it get bigger and better. Some of the ways to encourage owners are:

- Posting board meeting dates/time/location in the community and on their website urging owners to attend
- Listing board and committee members in the newsletter (recognition = encouragement)
- Selecting a "Volunteer of the Month" each month and having an article written about them and their contributions placed in the newsletter and on the community website
- Invite owners to submit information to the newsletter (providing a forum for positive community input translates into encouraging interest in the community)
- Create social events (and invite all owners to attend—nothing is more discouraging than having a social event and you are the only one there!)
- Have regular surveys in your newsletter and on your website (inviting the opinions of others encourages participation)

My previous book (Taking Control: Time Management and Communication Tools for Community Association Management) dealt with the relationship between effective communication and successful time management. I pointed out that by the effective use of the various communication tools at the disposal of management, a manager could drastically decrease the amount of time spent putting out unexpected fires (being reactive) and could increase the amount of time they spend actually accomplishing work that needs to be done (being proactive). Time spent being reactive results in consequences (working too late, having to continually play catch-up, disliking your job) while time spent being proactive produced rewards (not working too late, getting your action list completed, enjoying your work). I would argue that effective use of communication and communication tools have a similar effect upon creating community.

When communication is embraced by the board of directors and management, there is less time spent having to deal with issues of community apathy (non-compliance issues, quorum challenges at the annual meetings, committees without members, etc.) and more time spent enjoying the benefits of an active, engaged, caring community (attendance at board meetings and positive input, committees with active members, successful social events, active neighborhood watch programs—less community crime and increased compliance with community rules and regulations). To me, it is a no-brainer. As was mentioned before: Communication is the most effective means of empowering others and without empowerment you will never be able to lay the foundation for the community-consciousness necessary in order to create community.

Even though it should be glaringly obvious that any successful community association has to be committed to regular communication tools (meetings, committees, newsletters, websites) communication tools are often the first to be discontinued whenever the association experiences any kind of financial challenge as they are often viewed as non-essential expenses. During the recent economic recession (depression?), we have seen property values drop drastically. Foreclosures have become very commonplace in most every community association. As the ability to collect assessments has decreased, many boards have had to reduce the expenses that they have control over. Utility expenses, insurance costs and maintenance expenditures are beyond the board's control. What often happens is that the board begins to look for less expensive management and service vendors. But, the first thing to go are usually the communication tools—Newsletters and websites.

When times are hard and the association quits communicating with the owners, it makes things even tougher. Less expensive management usually results in less quality management (you don't get what you don't pay for!) and less expensive landscaping service, pool service, security service usually results in shoddy service (you get what you pay for!). If communication tools have to be discontinued, or scaled back, then the board needs to consider alternative communication options in order to keep the membership informed, educated and encouraged. Some of those options include:

- More community social events (potlucks, clean-up days, block parties)
- Augmenting board meetings with regularly scheduled "Town Hall Meetings" where, in an informal atmosphere, the board can address questions, provide information and share ideas about upcoming projects. Keep in mind that these informal meetings are not held to conduct business or make decisions.
- Install bulletin boards in the community on which notices can be placed regarding association issues
- Have volunteers go door-to-door in order to survey the owners, provide information, or invite owners to a community event.
- Put more emphasis on existing programs, such as neighborhood watch, in order to provide owners with opportunities to remain involved.

There are always other options in order to keep the communication channels open within any community, regardless of the financial condition of the association. Too often, however, once the newsletter is discontinued or the website is shut down, boards retreat back into silence and any community-building gains are quickly lost. Flexibility, creativity and persistence are key in overcoming any challenging situation. Creating community is no different. If we revisit the ultimate formula for empowerment (finding out what owners think about the issues; letting them participate in decisions about those issues; and, getting out of the way and letting them contribute to resolution of those issues) then we have to be able to continue to communicate even when the normal communication channels have shutdown.

The third face of empowerment is the face of communication. In a later chapter we will discuss the effective use of the communication tools available in order to help create community.

Developmental Stages: Building Blocks of Community

It is important to remember that creating community involves a series of developmental stages. Creating community does not happen overnight. Changing perceptions, earning the trust of the community, helping people understand the common values that everyone in the community share and realizing actual engagement and participation in the community all happen over time.

Based on his experience with community building workshops, M. Scott Peck, reknowned pyschiatrist and author, says that community building typically goes through four stages:

- **Pseudocommunity**: This is a stage where the members pretend to have a *bon homie* with one another, and cover up their differences, by acting as if the differences do not exist. Pseudocommunity can never directly lead to community, and it is the job of the person guiding the community building process to shorten this period as much as possible.
- **Chaos**: When pseudocommunity fails to work, the members start falling upon each other, giving vent to their mutual disagreements and differences. This is a period of chaos. It is a time when the people in the community realize that differences

cannot simply be ignored. Chaos looks counterproductive but it is the first genuine step towards community building.

- **Emptiness**: After chaos comes emptiness. At this stage, the people learn to empty themselves of those ego related factors that are preventing their entry into community. Emptiness is a tough step because it involves the death of a part of the individual. But, Scott Peck argues, this death paves the way for the birth of a new creature, the Community.

- **True Community**: Having worked through emptiness, the people in community are in complete empathy with one another. There is a great level of tacit understanding. People are able to relate to each other's feelings. Discussions, even when heated, never get sour, and motives are not questioned.

Using this model, many of your community associations are probably mired in the "chaos" stage and you are looking for a way out . . . read on . . .

The **Forming—Storming—Norming—Performing** model of group development was first proposed by Bruce Tuckman in 1965, who maintained that these phases are all necessary and inevitable in order for a community to grow, to face up to challenges, to tackle problems, to find solutions, to plan work, and to deliver results. The Boy Scouts adopted this model of group development. Following is a definition of this model:

Forming: In the first stages of community building, the *forming* of the community takes place. The individual's behavior is driven by a desire to be accepted by the others, and avoid controversy or conflict. Serious issues and feelings are avoided, and people focus on being busy with routines, such as community organization, who does what, when to meet, etc. But individuals are also gathering information and impressions—about each other, and about the scope of the task and how to approach it. This is a comfortable stage to be in, but the avoidance of conflict and threat means that not much actually gets done.

The community meets and learns about the opportunities and challenges, and then agrees on goals and begins to tackle the tasks. Community members tend to behave quite independently. They may be motivated but are usually relatively uninformed of the issues and objectives of the team. Community members are usually on their best behavior but very focused on themselves. Mature community members begin to model appropriate behavior even at this early phase.

The forming stage of any community is important because, in this stage, the members of the community get to know one another, exchange some personal information, and make new friends. This is also a good opportunity to see how each member of the community works as an individual and how they respond to pressure.

Storming: Every group will next enter the *storming* stage in which different ideas compete for consideration. The community addresses issues such as what problems they are really supposed to solve, how they will function independently and together and what leadership model they will accept. Community members open up to each other and confront each other's ideas and perspectives. In some cases *storming* can be resolved quickly. In others, the team never leaves this stage. The maturity of some team members usually determines whether the team will ever move out of this stage. Some team members will focus on minutiae to evade real issues.

The *storming* stage is necessary to the growth of the community. It can be contentious, unpleasant and even painful to members of the community who are averse to conflict. Tolerance of each community member and their differences should be emphasized. Without tolerance and patience the community building will fail. This phase can become destructive to the community and will lower motivation if allowed to get out of control. Some communities will never develop past this stage.

Norming: The community manages to have one goal and come to a mutual plan for the community at this stage. Some may have to give up their own ideas and agree with others in order to make the community function. In this stage, all community members take the responsibility and have the ambition to work for the success of the community's goals.

Performing: It is possible for some communities to reach the *performing* stage. These high-performing communities are able to function as a unit as they find ways to get the job done smoothly and effectively. Community members have become interdependent. By this time, they are motivated and knowledgeable and understand that "together we're better." The community members are now competent, autonomous and able to handle the decision-making process without supervision. Dissent is expected and allowed as long as it is channeled through means acceptable to the community.

Even the most high-performing communities will revert to earlier stages in certain circumstances. Many long-standing communities go through these cycles many times as they react to changing circumstances. For example, a change in leadership may cause the community to revert to *storming* as the new people challenge the existing norms and dynamics of the community.

Keep in mind that in every model of the stages of community-building there are built-in assumptions that may and may not be appropriate for the community association. The board of directors themselves have to create their own sense of community with each other before they can effectively reach out and inspire others to follow their example.

The stages of community-building can just as easily be applied to board-building as the individual members of the board work to come together and begin to work as a cohesive unit. I propose the following model of the specific stages of development within a community association:

Bonding: The *bonding* stage consists of the time required for the board to work together as one cohesive unit. Goals are set, roles are defined and the hierarchy within the board is created. Unless this stage occurs—and in many community associations it does not—then nothing will be created except division within the community because the people leading the community are divided amongst themselves. Some of the activities that the board should consider doing in order to make sure that this stage is completed are:

- Organizing a social gathering of the board prior to any formal meeting in order for each board member to get to know one another, their significant others and to share their backgrounds. Understanding what each person brings to the board table is essential to successful board dynamics and creates the foundation for understanding future opinions and positions.
- Conduct an informal brainstorming session at which each member shares their vision of the community, ideas for future projects, opinions on solving existing community issues and individual goals they have while on the board. At the end of the session, begin work on a mission statement for the current board—what it is they want to accomplish and how—outside of their legally mandated mission (protect, preserve & enhance common assets).
- At board meetings, make sure every board member is given an opportunity to voice their opinions and suggested course of action regarding whatever issue is at hand.

- Revisit the mission statement often to ensure that the board is continuing in the direction that everyone wanted it to.

Building: The *building* stage is the most dynamic because it creates the means by which everything the board wants to create will happen. Once the board has jelled into a cohesive unit, it becomes time to create the vehicles to bring others on board. Some of the issues dealt with in the building stage are:

- Selecting management and service vendors
- Identifying and creating committees and programs the board requires in order to accomplish their goals
- Creating and implementing a communication plan (newsletter schedule, website features, bulletin board responsibilities, etc.)
- Setting up a yearly calendar that defines when community issues need to be addressed (i.e., tree trimming, audit, disclosure mailings, maintenance projects, etc.)
- Plan initial social events (garage sales, meet & greet the board, community clean-up day, neighborhood watch program orientation, etc.).

Inviting: The *inviting* stage is the period of time that encompasses utilization of all the tools created and implemented in the *building* stage. This stage focuses on reinforcing the transparency of the community and laying the foundation of empowerment by providing opportunities for the owners to get involved. Some of the activities that come out of this stage are:

- Volunteers are recruited for committees
- Owners are urged to attend board meetings
- Newsletters are sent out
- Websites are updated

- Social events are announced

Listening: Once the board has the attention of the owners and there is an increase in participation, the *listening* stage is vital in order to keep their interest and reinforce the new found perception that the board (and community) truly care about what ALL the owners think. Without the *listening* stage, the owners will slowly retreat back into their shells, so to speak. Some of the key activities of the *listening* stage are:

- Holding informal town hall meetings (outside of the board meeting) at which the board asks for input/comments/positive suggestions from the owners
- Providing surveys and comment sheets in the newsletter and website
- Encourage owners to attend the open forum session of the board meeting
- Have management follow up on suggetions/comments submitted with a thank you note
- Utilize committees in order to augment the decision-making process
- Ensure that management reports on all communications received from the owners

Doing: As important as listening is, if there are no actions implemented because of the listening, owners will quickly realize that no matter what they say or do, nothing is changing. The *doing* stage is characterized by activity, such as:

- Enforcing rules and regulations (especially those that are the cause of community-wide concern)
- Acting on committee suggestions
- Beginning maintenance projects that have a highly perceived value by the owners

- Publishing owner submitted articles in the newsletter and on the website
- Recognizing community volunteers and their contributions in the newsletter and on the website
- Ensure that social events are being planned (with the help of a social committee) on a regular basis
- Continue to solicit input from owners, management and vendors regarding their suggestions for improving the community

Even though there is continuity in the stages of every model of community/group/team building, each community will travel through each stage uniquely. The dynamics of a single-family home community are different than that of a condo association. What is important for a community made up of mostly older, retired couples is not the same as that of a community made up of younger, working couples with children in the home. The important thing to remember is that no matter what stage your community is going through, recognize where you are at and *put energy into continuing to move on*. Improvement, in all situations, depends upon change and moving on from where you are at now. Being aware of the unique character of your community and figuring out exactly what will work best for it, is a very important skill that will come when you are committed to community building.

When asked about the most effective method or technique of connecting with others in a meaningful way and of reducing conflicts with others, the Dali Lama said, " . . . dealing with others is a very complex issue. There is no way that you can come up with one formula that could solve all problems. It's a bit like cooking. If you are cooking a very delicious meal, a special meal, then there are various stages in the cooking. You may have to first boil the vegetables separately and then you have to fry them and then you combine them in a special way, mixing in spices and so on. And finally, the end result would be this delicious product. Similarly here, in order to be skillful in dealing with others, you need many factors. You can't just say, 'This is the method' or 'This is the technique.'"

The fourth face of empowerment is the face of developmental growth.

Respect/Trust

Assuming that your community association has embraced the faces of empowerment already described, there is one element that is necessary in order to ensure that community-consicious becomes the face of your community: Respect and the trust that goes along with that.

As is commonly taught, respect has to be earned and trust becomes the product of that respect. But, how does one earn respect in the community association arena when initial perceptions of the association (and those associated with it) are indifferent at best? It's like climbing a mountain on your knees, difficult and time-consuming. There are many things that can be done to earn the respect and trust of others, but they all boil down to being able to positively connect with others and their response to that connection. The great football coach, Vince Lombardi said, "It is essential to understand that battles are primarily won in the hearts of men. Men respond to leadership in a most remarkable way and once you have won his heart, he will follow you anywhere."

Here are some techniques that you—and other guiding members of your community—can elicit in order to earn that respect and the trust that follows it:

- Being able to view situations objectively
- Being able to appreciate the backgrounds of the people in your community
- Being able to remain honest in all of your dealings with people in your community
- Being humble in your contributions to the community

- Being patient when working with others in your community
- Being grateful for the contributions others make in your community
- Being able to treat others in your community with respect and trust

If you take all of those ingredients that contribute to earning respect and trust and mix them together, you get one fundamental behavior that describes them all: Kindness. Being kind is the best way to earn anyone's respect and trust. Let's look at each of those behaviors listed that sum up what it is to kind.

Being able to view situations objectively: Earlier, I introduced to you Lou Sifer, the homeowner who blamed the burglary of his home on the security service and the board of directors when, in fact, he left his garage door open and was ultimately responsible for what happened. He chose to view his situation *subjectively*. His perception is the only one that matters to him. Lou chooses to experience his world through the lens of his own experiences and what he values, believes, perceives and desires. It is like looking through a lens, but instead of seeing what the lens is pointed at, Lou sees only his reflection in the lens. Everyone has moments of uncomfortable subjectivity. Uncomfortable because whenever we expect others to behave as we want them to, or events to unfold as we desire, we are bound to be disappointed because that seldom happens. Many of us have to learn to have a more objective view of the world if we want to navigate more smoothly through the journey of life. Objectivity is the ability to perceive the world around you as it truly is, not prejudiced by your own values, beliefs, perceptions or desires. Unfortunately, recognizing the limiting quality of subjectivity takes a measure of objectivity to accomplish.

There is another wisdom tale in which seven blind men had a dispute as to the nature of what an elephant was. Unable to agree, they sought one out and each took hold of a different part of the elephant in order to prove their point. One took hold of the elephant's ear, and declared that elephants were clearly like parchment, thin and flexible. Another took hold of the elephant's tusk and disagreed, stating that he clearly could tell that elephants were like spears, sharp and pointed. Yet another, having taken hold of the elephant's trunk declared the others to have failed in their perceptions, declaring that elephants were clearly like snakes. And so it continued, with the other men each seizing a part of the Elephant, be it the legs, the tail, or the broad flanks and declaring that particular part to define the whole, never truly comprehending the true nature of the unique creature in whose presence they were standing.

So often it seems that such is the nature of human perception in general. We see the world through our own incomplete subjectivity, we perceive details and circumstances that are specific to us and our particular experience, culture and lifestyle, and mistake our perceptions for objective reality, which is far more complex than the simplified vision we create. As such, in a very real sense, we are blind, for we are unable to get beyond our limited perceptions to see the whole.

Choosing to look at situations and events through the clearer eyes of objectivity makes all of the other attributes of respect and trust possible. If for no other reason than being objective allows us to see the limitations of those around us and adjust our approach accordingly. There is never just one way to look at something—there are always different perspectives, meanings, and perceptions, depending on who is looking.

Being able to appreciate the backgrounds of the people in your community: Certainly there are elements of objectivity in this behavior, however it differs from being able to appreciate the backgrounds of others in its scope. Most people do not wear tags that tell you what life has given or taken away from them. To recognize that other people have different perceptions based upon their life experiences is important, but to understand what those experiences are is more powerful and requires another set of skills: being able to actively listen and being able to act empathetically.

When working with others, if we never actively listen, we never learn anything about those people. We all go through life creating many different stories to help us define who we are to ourselves and to others and we often share those stories in our daily conversations in order to strengthen, reinforce or justify our actions or opinions. When someone begins a sentence with "When I . . . ." or, "One time I . . ." you can rest assured that you are about to hear one of their life "stories." When that happens, pay attention. You are about to learn something important about their background and their values, beliefs and perceptions.

In addition, as is often the case within any community, we can learn about other people's backgrounds by listening to how other people talk about them. The person who shares an experience or a fact about a neighbor is giving you an insight. The key, again, is to be aware and file away all the information that you can learn and use it for our second skill in being able to appreciate the backgrounds of others: empathy.

In "The Art of Happiness" the Dali Lama discusses empathy: "I think that empathy is important not only as a means of enhancing compassion, but I think that generally speaking, when dealing with others on any level, if you're having some difficulties, it's extremely helpful to be able to try to put yourself in the other person's place and see how you would react to the situation. Even if you have no common experiences with the other person or have a very different lifestyle, you can try to do this through imagination. You may need to be slightly creative. This technique involves the capacity to *temporarily suspend insisting on your own viewpoint but rather to look from the other person's percpective, to imagine what would be the situation if you were in his shoes, how you would deal with this.* This helps you develop an awareness and respect for another's feelings, which is an imnportant factor in reducing conflicts and problems with other people."

Simply put, as the Dali Lama points out, empathy is the ability to put yourself in another's shores. This skill guarantees that you will be able to relate to others more authentically because your actions are based on a more honest, objective viewpoint.

Being able to remain honest in all of your dealings with people in your community: Arthur Ciaramicoli, psychologist, author and Harvard University instructor defines honesty as "the ability to see oneself clearly, to understand others accurately, and, above all, to communicate those perceptions in sensitive, tactful ways." (11) Just as being transparent in community association business contributes to creating community on an organizational level, honesty allows us to be transparent on an interpersonal level and results in the respect and trust of those we work with. If respect and trust are based upon lies or misconceptions, then that respect and trust is misplaced and will eventually be lost. No matter how uncomfortable being honest may be at times, to act honestly, according to Piero Ferrucci, "repects our own integrity and acknowledges in others the capacity to be competent and mature." That acknowledgement comes back in the form respect and trust, one of the faces of empowerment and essential in creating community.

To be honest also means to recognize when there is a problem and not pretend that nothing is wrong. If the board of directors and/or management fail to recognize a problem in the community that most of the owners plainly see, they are not being honest with either themselves or others. If we do not call the hard realities of our community by name, we live in a land of dreams and harmful illusions, neither of which contribute to community consciousness.

Acting honestly also requires that we recognize the positives that you and everyone else on the board and in the community bring to the community building effort. Often times we temper our enthusiasum, our creativity, our kindness when assuming our community role because we don't want to let it all hang out and put ourselves at risk of being seen as weak, or too emotional, or ridiculous. However, honesty requires that we share all of ourselves, not just that part of ourselves that is safe. Honesty is an attitude that is expressed in everything that we do and is recognized for what it is. There are no deceptions allowed because we want others to know we are who we say we are. How can we relate to others in a meaningful way if we can't be truthful with them? If we don't offer sincerity, how can we ask it in return? It is said that lying has a thousand faces and the truth only one. If we want to unite others we are going to have a much better chance of succeeding if we embrace honesty and everything that it entails.

Some things that can be done to promote acting honestly are:

- Frequently conduct community surveys in order to solicit perceptions and comments about the state of the community, both positive and negative
- Have each board member make a list of issues in the community that need addressing
- Have each board member make a list of the positives within the community
- Solicit input on the community from management and service vendors
- Publish highlights from each board meeting in the newsletter
- Establish a "Letters to the Editor" section in the newsletter and solicit contributions from all the owners
- Acknowledge issues that can be improved to owners in the newsletter and website and ask for suggestions on how to improve them

- Reply to every suggestion, letter and comment submitted by owners, thanking them for their input
- On a regular basis have board members evaluate the effectiveness of the board in keeping with its initial mission statement

Being humble in your contributions to the community: I am familiar with a community association whose board president insists upon being called "The Major." He even refers to himself in the third person as "The Major." He spent most of his adult life in the military and believes that a community association should be run like a military division with strict disipline, iron-fisted control and unwavering obedience by all residents. He personally takes credit for all community accomplishments and hand picks his fellow board members from among the weakest members of the community who clammer for any kind of recognition. Then, he strongarms the membership in order to gain control of their proxies and harasses any capable members who express an interest in being elected to the board until they realize it's not worth the trouble. Another hijacking and another community association with no interest in creating community. The Major has no desire whatsoever in empowering anyone other than himself and he takes every opportunity to crow about his ability to govern the community in the best way possible: his way. His boastfulness and swagger—his braggadocio—is guaranteed to keep most owners completely disinterested in their community association because if they start to look into it, they quickly become disgusted and avert their attention to other things in their lives that are not so frustrating. I could go on and on about the kind of abuses "The Major" inflicts upon his community, but I am sure you get the point: Excessive ego does not promote creating unity and it certainly does not attract respect or trust. In fact, the exact opposite is true. Empowering others means applauding *their* contributions and promoting *their* ideas and suggestions. It's not about 'me' it is about 'we'.

The plain truth is that if we are honest with ourselves, we quickly realize just how much we don't know and how much easier life becomes when you begin to look to others for guidance and advice, and to understand that there are experiences in life that are meant to teach us valuable life lessons. To be honest and know your own weaknesses and accept them, no matter how painful that may be. That is humility and humility is a very precious strength, especially in community building.

There is a Zen saying that states in the mind of a beginner there are infinite possibilities, but in the mind of an expert exist only a few. It is much better to embrace the mind of a beginner because you readily admit that you do not know much and are more open to learn. Despite your life experiences, whether you were the president of General Motors or an ambasador to France, humility renews who you are because it puts you in a position of infinite possibilities, of being able to perceive issues through the eyes of others, and to learn something new. It is putting yourself in a capacity to learn that expresses itself most favorably in the eyes of those around you and will earn you their deep respect.

A recent study has shown that, if you want to be at your best in learning, humility is your tool. The humblest students, who think they know the least, do more tests and research when given a problem, and prove to be more efficient than those who think they already have the answer. It is hardly surprising. A student who overestimates her own knowledge will fail the exam, just as a sportswoman who underestimates her competitors will lose, or the boardmember who knows what is best for their community will further divide it. Being humble means you work harder and you prepare yourself better.

A technique to use in order to foster humility when working with others is to always ask yourself, *"What is it that this person can teach me?"* In community building we are surrounded by people who can enrich our life through their experiences, feelings, ideas, dreams and values. All we have to do is remain open to that learning and to listen.

Be wary of anyone who overly pursues an important role within the community association hierarchy as it may indicate an unhealthy lack of humility required in creating community. When the role is important it can serve to hide weakness by providing fictitious strength. If I am board president, I am no longer the malcontent who cannot get along with his wife, or if I am the treasurer, I am no longer the struggling businessman who cannot pay his bills. Positions of power should be *given* to those that have earned the respect and trust of their neighbors, not taken by arrogant know-it-alls.

In an Afghan story, a king governs his country in a dictatorial and ruthless way. He commands his subjects and harasses them with unjust taxes, not caring for them—in his eyes they are mere pawns without faces. One day, he goes hunting and chases a gazelle. The gazelle runs fast, leading the king into unknown places, on and on til he is lost, right to the edge of the desert. The gazelle disappears and the king, disappointed, decides to go back, but because he has strayed so far, he is no longer sure of the way. A terrible dust storm blows for three days. He wanders without knowing where he is going. By the end of the storm, he is alone in the desert. He is lost. His clothes are torn to shreds, his face unrecognizable, distorted by fear and fatigue. He meets some nomads. When he tells them he is the king, they laugh, yet they help him, give him food, and tell him the way. With great effort the king returns to his palace, but the guards—his own guards—do not recognize him and do not let him in. They take him to be a poor crazed fool.

Bit by bit the king learns to live in poverty. He manages, but never without the help of others. One day someone offers him water to drink, another day someone else gives him food, or shelter, or work. And he, too, puts in effort. He helps whomever he can. Once he saves the life of a child trapped inside a house on fire. Another time he offers food to someone hungrier than he is. Slowly the king comes to understand that his subjects are people like him, and that in life, people must care for each other. He learns that life is more beautiful and interesting when we love and help one another. In the end, he realizes the time has come for him to return to his palace and reign again. But this time the king governs wisely and kindly because he has learned the priceless lesson of humility.

Humility places us in a state in which learning is possible. Because creating community is an on-going process that demands constant stewardship, the best stewards are the ones who are constantly learning new things about their community, their neighors, their roles and themselves . . . and the most valuable resources they have to facilitate that learning are their friends and neighbors within the community itself.

Being patient when working with others in your community: Because of erosion, the historic Cape Hatteras Lighthouse was in peril of washing into the Atlantic Ocean. So Congress appropriated $12 million for the National Park service to move it 2900 feet to safety. With a combination of care, expertise, patience and raw power, The Expert House Movers of Sharptown, Maryland moved the 208 foot tall, 9.7 million pound structure to its current home. The option of moving the lighthouse was first proposed in April of 1982, but the light wasn't lit at its new location until November 13, 1999. 17 years of study and 23 days of moving later. Why did it take so long? *Small things can be moved quickly, but big things take time.* Most people tend to overestimate what they can do in a week and underestimate what they can do in a lifetime. When creating community, patience is absolutely necessary because empowerment and uniting others is a HUGE undertaking. As I have tried to convey to you, the reader, there are many underlying elements that must be created and nurtured first before any real outward progress is made in community building.

We have access to instant information, music and books. We buy fast food through the drive-thru. We beep at the car in front of us as soon as the light turns green. Resolutions to problems or relationships are expected instantly. We want to see immediate results related to the turnaround of our economy, despite the fact that it took years to get to this state. We enter foreign countries and expect to immediately change their culture. If a CEO is put in place and doesn't demonstrate an immediate turn-around, they take a walk through the revolving door and someone new is put in place. Unfortunately, we try to live our fast paced lifestyle in what is naturally a slow paced world. Creating community is no different except that if we assume that the majority of owners would rather forget about their roles within their community association, and remain indifferent and uninvolved. Apathy should never be confused with patience. However, when the sleeping giant wakes up and realizes that things are awry, change cannot happen fast enough. Without the fundamentals of creating community underneath any community leadership, any hopefully long-lasting change is bound to be short-lived and and can begin a viscious cycle of changes just for the sake of change, hoping that an effective formula for creating a strong, vibrant, active community can be stumbled upon . . . accidently.

A good lesson on this subject is reflected is the story of the Chinese Bamboo Tree. It seems that this tree when planted, watered, and nurtured for an entire growing season doesn't outwardly grow as much as an inch. Then, after the second growing season, a season in which the farmer takes extra care to water, fertilize and care for the bamboo tree, the tree still hasn't sprouted. So it goes as the sun rises and sets for four solid years. The farmer has nothing tangible to show for all of his labor trying to grow the tree. Then, along comes year five.

In the fifth year that Chinese bamboo tree seed finally sprouts and the bamboo tree grows up to eighty feet in just one growing season! Or so it seems . . . .

Did the little tree lie dormant for four years only to grow exponentially in the fifth? Or, was the little tree growing underground, developing a root system strong enough to support its potential for outward growth in the fifth year and beyond? The answer is, of course, obvious. Had the tree not developed a strong unseen foundation it could not have sustained its life as it grew.

The same is true for our community building efforts. Community leaders, who patiently work teaching owners the value of community and becoming involved while overcoming adversity and challenge, grow a strong internal foundation. Had the Chinese bamboo farmer dug up his little seed every year to see if it was growing, he would have stunted the tree's growth. We ask our owners to have patience as we work on creating community. Much better lesson if we're demonstrating that behavior ourselves. True and lasting change, the kind that helps unite people and creates community, takes continual effort . . . and time!

Here is a poem by Henry Wadsworth Longfellow that is as true today as it was when he wrote it over 100 years ago:

> "The heights by great men reached and kept
> Were not attained by sudden flight,
> But they, while their companions slept,
> Toiled ever upward through the night."

Patience, as a group dynamic, is the water that creating community needs in order to steadily grow. Patience, on an interpersonal level, is the ground that community is grown upon. When working with others, on an interpersonal level, patience usually needs to be practiced when dealing with difficult people. There is an old English proverb that states "Patience wears away stones." The only effective way to deal with insufferable people is with patience. If done skillfully, honestly and with sensitivity, you can wear away their obnoxiousness and even help them realize a more healthy, productive way to communicate their needs to others.

Patience is also the skill of understanding and respecting the rhythms that community associations must operate on and the rhythms of owners who have no such understanding. Whenever anyone (ourselves included) push their rhythms upon others, causing others to feel discomfort, they exhibit impatience. An example is the owner who calls management day in and day out to complain about the tree that is blocking their view and demands that it be trimmed immediately. Or, the owner who continually stops the board president as she is walking her dog in the community to find out what is being done about all the unsupervised children that play in the community. As previously mentioned, we are a culture of immediate gratification. If we can't have it NOW, we throw a hissy fit. When the hissy fit is based upon misinformation, misunderstanding or ignorance, it's easy to dismiss the initial concern but nearly impossible to ignore the consequences: a sense of being violated.

Many owners may not understand (due to a lack of regular communication regarding community maintenance projects) that tree trimming is done seasonally on a predetermined schedule and subject to an inspection by the landscape committee and their recommendations. Is the board going to abandon their annual tree trimming schedule (alter the community rhythm) in order to satisfy the demands of the difficult owner? Hardly. However, if that owner is dealt with through a patient attempt to invite them into a more constructive conversation that would inform them of community schedules and why they exist and urge their involvement in helping the community by volunteering for the landscape committee, then not only can the problem (difficult owner) be solved, but it can help make the community stronger (by adding a committee volunteer). Once informed with respect, most difficult owners tend to be more sympathetic to the demands of community association management and any negotiations required to solve community problems can be more productive. In community building, sympathetic understanding can be the beginning of active participation in the community building effort. It all begins with being patient when dealing with difficult people: those people who have no patience.

Exercise: The purpose of this exercise is to identify your primary method of responding to difficult people. Each of us has a tendency to respond to difficult people in a particular way. Think back to your last few encounters with difficult people. What did you do?

- Did you avoid dealing with the problem or pretend everything was fine?
- Did you make nice and actively try to please the other person?
- Did you think about leaving or actually leave?
- Did you think about getting even or engaging in revenge?
- Did you fight back through institutional or legal avenues?
- Did you try to change what the other person was doing?
- Did you ask yourself what you could be learning from the situation?

Each approach has its advantages and disadvantages. If you have a tendency to rely on a particular option, consider whether the option is the one that serves you best.

Being grateful for the contributions others make in your community: On our journey towards community, practicing gratefulness will ensure that our trip is a happy and successful one. Maintaining an 'attitude of gratitude' allows us to appreciate what others bring to our community building efforts and that appreciation will encourage more giving. It is the law of attraction at work. When we are grateful for and appreciate what we have, we manifest more of what we are grateful for. When we are grateful for the time, energy, experience and skills that every owner brings to creating community, we are ensured to attract more people to volunteer their time, energy, experience and skills. The result is that our community building efforts will continue to grow exponentially. As the poet, William Blake, wrote "Gratefulness is heaven itself."

The dynamic at work is a simple one. When we empower others to identify and research community issues, listen to their comments and suggestions, act on their advice and give them credit and acknowledgement (whether a committee or an individual), privately and in public, we reinforce more continued involvement within the community. Not just from those who have already contributed but from others who are witness to the community's acts of gratefulness. In community building, the attitude of gratitude begins the process, but acts of gratefulness seal the deal.

John F. Kennedy said, "As we express our gratitude, we must never forget that the highest appreciation is not to utter words, but to live by them." It is not enough just to feel gratitude and thank those that donate their time to our community—whether it is serving on a committee, attending a board meeting or volunteering to be a neighborhood watch block captain—the board of directors must act on their input and advice. Some suggestions are no-brainers, others may be a bit more difficult to follow due to legal, financial or moral considerations. However, there is always something that can be done that reflects the spirit of the input provided.

At the beginning of our efforts to create community, it is a feeling of discontent that motivates a desire to change. There is a desire to criticize others, look for what is wrong and feel defeated. Community cannot grow in that kind of environment. The antidote for being discontent is to adopt a philosophy of gratitude. Even in the most dysfunctional of communities, there are positive elements. Once those positive elements are recognized and appreciated, once we see value in even the most unremarkable situations, we begin to bring more positives into the community building equation and we are that much closer to our goal. One of the ways to build gratitude in a community is to remind others of how much everyone's community building efforts have achieved and how far they have traveled from the point at which they started. What makes gratitude work is recognition of the difference between what is and what was. If things were not so bad, improvement would not feel so good. You appreciate good health after overcoming sickness, appreciate friendship more after making up after a fight, love life more when we are close to death. The collective consciousness of the community is no different than the individual consciousnesses that it is made up of. That is why it is so important to regularly list the accomplishments of the board of directors and the committees in communications to the owners. Knowing what is being done in order to better serve common interests feeds gratitude and gratitude is contagious. When we see what is good around us and point it out to others, they become able to see it too and also share it with others, who share it with others, who share it with others, etc.

Some of the activities that help promote an attitude of gratitude are:

- Make a mental list of those all the good things you see in your community
- Write down the list you just created, let those people who may be responsible for those positive things know how much you appreciate their efforts
- Recruit a volunteer photographer who can take 'before' and 'after' photos of maintenance projects and publish them in the newsletter and website

- Create an 'Owner of the Month' award that is given to recognize community volunteers and highlight them in the newsletter and on the website
- Invite positive comments from owners regarding completed community improvement projects and publish them in the newsletter and on the website
- Have a yearly community-wide celebration that honors community volunteers
- Have management track the names of owners who contact them each week and the reason for the contact and follow-through with postcards thanking them for their comments/suggestions/ requests/report.

Being able to treat others in your community with respect and trust: What do you think it would do to our community building efforts if we treated the owners as 'The Major' does, as infantry soldiers and worker bees who are expected to blindly obey his demands and stay out of the way so that the people (him) who know what they are doing can do their job? Now, what do you think it would do to our community building efforts if we treated all owners with respect, honored their contributions and trusted their commitment to helping create community? If you put energy into the other five techniques to gain the trust and respect of others, then treating others with respect and trust is a by-product of that energy and something that happens naturally.

No one wants to be seen as less than they are. From the viewpoint of the community building dynamic, when owners either view their community leaders as buffons or, worse yet, as nobodies, then that is showing a definite lack of respect. When community leaders believe that the owners are obstacles in their way, to be dismissed and avoided, that also is an example of a lack of respect. Both of those examples are unacceptable in creating community.

There are several simple techniques that can be employed by community leaders in order to show respect to the owners they serve. One of the simpliest is to have board members greet those owners who attend board meetings. Standing by the door and introducing themselves, having owners sign in with their address and then asking them if they would like water or coffee (which should be available) and engaging them in introductory conversation speaks to respect. Using the sign-in sheet, management should follow through and send a note thanking the owner for attending (or have them provide their email address and email them). It doesn't matter if they are there to crucify the board due to some perceived lack of leadership or error in judgement, what does matter is that whatever the issue is, it mattered enough for them to attend the meeting. If any complaint is handled correctly, you can probably even get them to volunteer to serve on a committee that can address their concerns. The board should make every effort to recognize and welcome every owner that attends a meeting or community event. Nothing is more disrespectful than ignoring someone.

Respect is not only about 'seeing' someone, recognizing their contributions and membership in the community, it is also about listening. How often have you been at a board meeting during the open forum session when, before an owner even finishes their comments, they are interrupted by a board member defending the board's position. That is the opposite of listening. True listening is allowing others to speak without interrupting them or paying total attention to what they are saying. One of the reasons that some boards dislike the requirement for open forum sessions is because they don't want to listen to the owners tell them their opinions about issues that they just don't understand, or so the board believes. Anyone who sits on a board that truly believes listening to owners does not make their job easier needs to resign. Listening shows respect and EVERYONE has something that they bring to the table and if you listen, you just might find a solution to a community-wide problem. To assume that anyone doesn't have something to contribute is ignorance personified.

In an African story, the spider Ananse is given a mission by the sky god to collect all the wisdom of the world and bring it back to him. In exchange, he will be called "the wisest of all time." "No problem," replies Ananse. "I'll do the lot in three days." He collects all the wisdom in the world and puts it in a large pot. Then, tying the pot to his back, he starts his climb to the sky, scaling very slowly a tall coconut tree whose top is lost in the clouds. When anyone offers him help, he refuses it: He wants to do the whole job by himself, wants to be the one and only keeper of wisdom. He is very proud of his task. From the ground, everyone follows him with baited breath. At the end, Ananse does it: He arrives in the sky with all of the wisdom of the earth. He has made it! What a triumph! What happiness! He lifts his eight legs high as a sign of victory. Alas! In doing this, he loses his grip and falls miserably to the ground. The pot breaks and the wisdom ends in a thousand pieces. Everyone wants these precious fragments and runs to get them: They are so interesting, so beautiful! And from that day, no one has a monopoly on wisdom. Everybody has a piece of it. Even the most ignorant, downtrodden, thick-headed, or apparently less-gifted have a piece of wisdom. Everyone has something interesting and original to say.

There is a practice that many groups employ that helps their members learn how to listen effectively. It would work great at board or committee orientation meetings because it helps us understand just how tempting it is to speak without listening. The exercise goes like this: Take a ball and put it in the middle of the group. Whoever wants to talk takes the ball and says what she wants to say. The others listen, and no one may speak unless she has the ball. When she has finished, she puts the ball back in the center and after a bit of silence, during which everybody digests what has just been said, someone else takes the ball. And so it goes on. Engaging a group in this exercise shows us how listening forces us to slow our pace, to consider meditatively, because true understanding requires pause and commitment.

Respect is also a necessary condition of all conflict resolution, and creating community demands effective means of resolving conflict. To resolve conflicts, the first step is to help the sides state their positions clearly and recognize the point of view and demands of the other. This is respect: the full acknowledgement of oneself and the other. Conflict resolution by way of respect and listening is the most efficient and elegant way to settle disputes. At times there is going to be irrationality, quarrelsomeness and/or rigidity at play and sometimes it does not work, but it is a useful starting point.

Finally, respect is all about being non-judgemental. Judgement is often linked to the desire to control. We want to give advice, tell people what is best for them, how to manage their lives, save them. How often have you had someone tell you what to eat, what books to read, how to use your time, or what God to believe in. Unfortunately, there are always some people who volunteer to serve on boards or committess that would be considered control-freaks, masters of judging others. They want to be in charge, assume they know what is best for everyone and believe that without their involvement, everything would fall apart. The mythical image of Procrustes' bed is a perfect example of this idea. This terrible man would make people lie on his bed, If they fit exactly, they were lucky. If they were too long, he would cut off their feet, and if they were too short, he would stretch them till they were the right size. The horror of Procrustes describes well the horror of those who want to interfere with other people's lives. At some time or another, we are all tempted to shape others the way we want them to be. Respect is also about tolerance, not judgement.

The last face of empowerment is the face of respect.

COMMUNICATION TOOLS

The Voice of Empowerment

The way you get meaning into your life is to devote yourself to loving others, devote yourself to your community around you, and devote yourself to creating something that gives you purpose and meaning.

—**Mitch Albom**

By now we should have a pretty good idea about what community looks like and some of the thought processes that are required in order to contribute to the community building effort. It begins with you and, through a series of deliberate and focused actions, others begin to change their perceptions, adopt community-consciousness and start to contribute their energy to help make the community better. Some owners reflect that contribution by volunteering to serve on a committee or the board of directors. Other owners decide to start attending community social events, join neighborhood watch and/or pay more attention to what is going on around them within the community. Still other owners will do nothing particularly outstanding. They will simply reflect their contribution by choosing to comply with community rules, reading correspondences from the community association and participating in the Annual Meeting by sending in their proxy and voting. There are many ways for owners to help create community and each one should be valued and positively reinforced.

The progression from dysfunctional to functional has many elements but there is one element that makes all the other community building efforts possible: Communication. Without communication and the communication tools at your disposal, community is impossible to achieve. After all, it takes communication to inform others. Without information, we don't know, we cannot have a conversation about community. We have already discussed many of the characteristics of communication: honesty, empathy, listening, etc. What we are going to look at now are the specific kinds of communication tools available to us today to in order to express the voice of community and begin that conversation.

In May 2009 I was interviewed for an article published in New England Condominium magazine about building community through communication. In the article I tried to emphasize the importance of boards utilizing "every communication tool available" in order to flatten the hierarchy and show the community that the board cares, that "they don't lord over other people, they actually want the best interests of the entire community, and don't have any specific personal agendas they're trying to achieve." The results of such a commitment were exemplified by a condominium association in Connecticut. The author of the article, Jonathan Barnes, interviewed the new board president. After what was a divisive battle within the community that resulted in a new board being elected, the key to healing the wounds of the community was communication. The board authorized a regular newsletter, overhauled their website and, in order to help overcome the sense of distrust, posted meeting minutes and community financials on it. Contact information for all the board and committees were published in the newsletter and reports on current maintenance projects were also included. The new board also created a social committee and a welcoming committee to build up a sense of community. The key to his community's healing, said the new president, was "openness, open communication and transparency."

It doesn't have to take a divisive battle between the forces of good and evil to realize that a community is wounded and needs help. In fact, I would guess that the fundamental polarizing issues are the same for most community associations as they were for the condominium association in Connecticut: Owners not knowing what is going on and the board unwilling to adapt to the needs of the community by embracing more open and honest communication. Every community association has wounds of some sort or another. But, regardless of the cause, the remedy is always the same: Communication!

When a community association decides that enough is enough and elects a board that promises to heal whatever the longstanding wounds within the community are, creating an effective communication plan requires that those wounds be named so that they can be specifically addressed and exorcized. For example, in order to keep from having to raise monthly assessments, for years a board of directors fails to adequately fund the reserves, instead choosing to use funds on operating expenses (landscape maintenance, management, water, insurance, etc.). As the years passed, it became time to replace roofs and repair the streets. However, since there was no money in the reserves, they had to pass a substantial special assessment in order to pay for the repairs. Since the owners had no idea that the money that should have been used for funding the reserves was being spent elsewhere, the news of a special assessment came as a shock. As the owners began to look into it, the board became even more rigid and opaque. When a group of owners finally found out what had been going on, they were furious and went door to door to let everyone else know that instead of having to pay a few dollars more each month for the past several years, they were now going to have to lay down some serious coin because of the actions of the current board. Friends of the current board rallied behind them and the disgruntled owners formed an informal ad hoc committee to oust the current board, thus dividing the community and creating a lot of anger and chaos. In the end, a new board was elected but the community remained divided and alienated from each other, hardly the scenario for community building.

However, the new board of directors took the time and energy to identify—to name—the true source of the community's woes and based on that process began to initiate reforms to make sure that the reserves began to be funded and owners kept informed about the financial condition of the association. In addition, an aggressive communication plan was implemented and new committees were formed, all for the purpose of healing the wounds caused by the actions of the previous board and the resulting reactions of disgruntled owners when they found out about those actions.

This is an example of a board being aware of what needed to be done in order to heal their community. However, that is not always the case. As John Bradshaw, author, theologian, management consultant and speaker, writes in "Healing the Shame that Binds You", toxic shame can result in a breakdown of the family system and keep you from going forward in your life. Toxic shame within the group/community dynamic is the collective effect of dealing with a dysfunctional leadership style that manifests itself individually as feelings of apathy, disinterest and frustration. Community association leaders can choose to increase toxic shame within their community by the way they relate and communicate (or not communicate) with the owners. Healing toxic shame requires identifying it exists, embracing it as a condition of powerlessness and taking action (empowering others) in order to transform it into a positive affect. Dynamically, toxic shame in a community results in incommunicability—there is no communicative interaction between anyone. Healing toxic shame requires understanding how it came about and healing those causes. To lead others from apathy to action, disinterest into participation and frustration into enjoyment, increased communication is the path to take.

Let's take a closer look at some of the communication tools that are available to community associations and how they can be effectively utilized in creating community: Newsletters, websites and social networks.

NEWSLETTERS

The Community Associations Institute (CAI) published a magazine called 'Common Ground' and in it they stated: "The newsletter is a community association's most valuable communications tool. It is the primary information link with homeowners, the best and most consistent way to keep owners informed of the association's activities". (3) Even with the advent of the internet and the use of websites for disseminating information, the newsletter continues to be the "best and most consistent way to keep owners informed of association activities." Why? Everyone has a mailbox (or should!) and receives mail, so a newsletter is guaranteed to reach every member and resident of a community association. Secondly, websites are passive and newsletters are aggressive, meaning that websites sit out in cyberspace and wait for someone to visit them. Websites do not go into people's homes and invite usage (spam aside!). Newsletters are sent out and received by everyone and do indeed invite the reader to participate in reading them simply by being mailed and received.

Newsletters function in a complimentary role to the website. The newsletter should be the primary source of referrals to the community association website. The website should exist in order to provide even greater information, communication and education to the members if only because of the amount of content it is able to provide in relation to a newsletter. However, the aggressive nature of the newsletter provides a community association website with a very effective marketing tool. Any successful communication program must have both a regular newsletter and a community website. One without the other decreases the effectiveness of both.

In order for a website to be effective it must be used and if no one ever hears about the site, then no one is ever going to use it. In addition to some of its other important functions, newsletters serve a very important marketing function for the community website. Through the reminders provided by regular newsletters and articles explaining the features and use of the community website, members will come to not only realize that they have a site, but how to use it and will visit it often, especially when it is used in the complimentary function briefly introduced above.

I certainly don't intend to get into a 'newsletter vs. website' debate because, as I just mentioned, a successful communication program needs both. However, it is very important to keep in mind the importance of the newsletter, especially in this day of the paperless internet and the desire to reduce extra costs. If every community association published a newsletter on a regular basis, then such an argument might have more merit because a culture of communication would already exist within the community association. The fact is, very few community associations utilize newsletters in the most effective means possible, if at all. Because of that, the goal of this section is to discuss the philosophy and merits of the community association newsletter so that a culture of communication can be created and such an argument can be more taken up more effectively in the future.

If owners and residents are informed of association issues, maintenance schedules, financial conditions and educated on their responsibilities as members of the association on a regular basis, there is going to be less confusion, more understanding and more support for decisions made by the board. Increased participation in association-related activities (such as board and committee meetings, social events and neighborhood watch programs) and a reduction in the number of "what the heck is going on here" calls to management are the more measurable behaviors that result in increasing effective communication. Less measurable but more significantly, is the sense of community that results in that increased participation.

Creating A Successful Newsletter

Now, let's get down to the best ways to create an effective newsletter. The best newsletters have four major components to them that increase their perceived value (how important the newsletter is to the community association members). Those components are: informational; educational; communicative; and, service-oriented.

Informational: The informational component consists of the articles that inform owners about what is going on within the community and association. Board meeting notices and highlights, notices of upcoming maintenance projects, updates on current maintenance projects, president's letters, committee reports, social event calendars, any kind of article that has a "what" element to it: What is going on.

Educational: The educational component is made up of those articles that have a "why" element: Why does the association do this? For example, articles explaining community rules would be considered educational if they not only remind residents of a particular rule or regulation but also explain why it is important that it be complied with. When you tell residents to clean up after their dog "because we told you to" it isn't going to go over very well. But when you explain that not only does it help keep our community clean and help protect the curb appeal of the community (which in turn helps protect property values), but that dog feces is the number one transmitter of canine diseases and by picking up after your dog you are doing your part to protect the health of the community canine population, then it gets the message across in a positive manner.

Other examples of the educational component are articles explaining some of the various issues that the association board of directors must make decisions upon either presently or in the future. Topics such as reserve funds, reserve studies, budgeting, rules enforcement, assessment collection policy, board meeting conduct and insurance are excellent to use for educational articles. Telling the members 'why' the board has to do what it does goes a long way in increasing understanding and support within the association and unites owners in that understanding—the crux of creating community.

Communicative: The communicative component is the "who" sections of the newsletter: Who do you contact. Often these sections simply list the management company representatives such as the manager, assistant manager, customer service and accounts receivable personnel. Other important information include board member names, committee chair names and local civic contacts such as non-emergency numbers for police and fire departments, utility company phone numbers, security service and cable television information. Surveys and requests for information from owners and residents are also parts of the communicative component.

Service-Oriented: For many residents, the service-oriented component is the most important element of the newsletter. These are the resident classified advertising, display ads or information about local businesses and services that many newsletters should include in order to add another dimension of service to the members of the community: the ability to sell their services and products to members of their own community. Newsletters that my company (Community Association Publishing Services) publish for community associations offer residents the opportunity to submit a 30 word classified ad for publication in each issue free of charge. A good measuring stick on how many people are actually reading the newsletter is by the number of people who submit a free classified ad.

By providing elements other than strictly community association issues within an association newsletter, the community association is able to expand the degree of interest that the newsletter will have. More owners and residents will view the newsletter as a valuable resource if the information included in it is relevant to their interests. The more valuable the newsletter is perceived as being, the more impact it will have, even though there is other information in it besides just community association-related issues, those association-related issues will carry more weight.

Below are some suggestions for ensuring that your community association newsletter becomes an effective communication tool and encourages community building:

Board submitted articles: Have management add a 'newsletter items' section to every board meeting agenda so that the board can provide input—and hopefully articles—to the next upcoming newsletter.

Use surveys to solicit feedback and generate interest: Probably the best resource the board of directors has to help them determine what issues are of interest within a community are the residents themselves. By including cut-out survey forms that residents can mail back to the manager along with their assessment payment, not only will the board be able to stay on top of community 'hotspots,' but the residents will feel as if their opinions and observations actually matter—which is an important element in creating community. Nothing encourages interest more than asking someone what they think about an issue. When the board develops a habit of going out to the community and soliciting opinions about association issues, they are increasing interest in the community. Increased interest leads to increased participation almost every time.

Used in conjunction with a community website, the newsletter can be used to announce online surveys as well. I work with many managers who include a general communication survey in nearly every newsletter and others who tailor each survey to correspond to an upcoming association issue so that the board of directors has a feel for how the community feels about it.

It is also a good idea to send a brief note, or email, to the residents who respond to the survey. Such positive feedback reinforces the chances that those people will respond again and also increase the perception that the board of directors and management are open to community feedback. Nothing turns off the communication channels or destroys any community building efforts faster than the belief that no one is listening.

Collect articles of interest: In between newsletter publication periods, always keep an eye out for informative articles that may have a special relevance for specific associations. Articles on pest control, community safety, gardening tips, or any number of homeowner-related issues are excellent additions to any newsletter. Remember that association members have a wide range of interests and roles besides being a member of their community association, as we have previously detailed. The more of those interests that you can touch upon in a newsletter, the more interest you will generate in the newsletter as a whole. Help the newsletter become a resource for community-living as well as an information and communication tool.

If you don't run across informational articles that you would like to add to a newsletter in your daily reading, perform internet searches on a topic using a search engine and see what is out there on the internet. They don't call it the "information superhighway" for nothing.

There are boards of directors that prefer not to include anything other than association-related news in newsletters for fear that anything else will dilute the importance of the association news presented. I've probably touched on that subject enough, but again, there is more to your member's lives than their community association and if you want to impact behavior or attitude regarding their association, you must earn their interest. Presenting wide ranges of information in each newsletter attempts to do just that.

Recruit owners to serve on a newsletter committee: Just as surveys are a great way to get a feel for what issues the members of a community feel are important to them, so is having an active newsletter committee made up of members of the community. These people live within the association and can provide valuable insight into how the community is feeling about various issues. A productive newsletter committee can do as little as simply provide someone on-property to collect information from other homeowners, to more extensive involvement such as coordinating community advertising, attend board/committee meetings, reporting on them, and taking responsibility for a majority of the newsletter content.

The key to recruiting and maintaining newsletter committee members is to keep their responsibilities to a minimum in order to keep them going for the long haul. Remember, their most important value to the board is to provide another set of eyes and ears within the community in order to make sure that the newsletters remain fresh and relevant to the community members. They don't necessarily have to attend meetings, solicit advertising or write all the articles in order to accomplish that. I've seen some good newsletter committee members hang it up only because they were expected to do everything. The more people within the community who can share the newsletter responsibilities the more successful newsletter committees are.

Emphasize the positive: I can't even begin to tell you how many articles that I have seen included in newsletters that sound more like scolding than enlightening residents. They usually sound something like this: *If residents do not start to pick up their dog's poop and disposing of it properly then the board of directors is going to have no choice but to raise your monthly assessments in order to pay for professional clean up. You don't have to be a rocket scientist to remember to put a plastic baggie in your pocket before taking your dog on a walk and using it to pick up the poop with. No one likes piles of poop on their living room carpet, why would anyone feel any differently about it on their lawn? Come on, get with it everyone!*

Now, to the reader the message is clear: Hey, stupid! Clean up your dog's poop or else! I don't know about you, but I usually don't respond in a positive manner with such negative direction. In fact, I'm more likely to become insulted and let those passive-aggressive tendencies come to the forefront of my behavior, start feeding my dog more fiber and let Fido poop anywhere he damn well pleases. Instead of helping solve a problem, by presenting it in a negative manner all that is going to be accomplished could just be a community-wide campaign to establish monuments of poop everywhere. No one likes being told what to do. That is one of the biggest challenges of community association management. With so many rules and restrictions, the owners become overly sensitive to expressing their own individuality and freedom and will often do everything they can to protest what they perceive as an attack on their 'castle'—their home. Sure they are legally obligated to conform to the governing documents and rules and regulations, but there are much better ways to obtain compliance than by the force of negative persuasion. You get what you give. If you want angry, resentful residents, present the issues in an angry, resentful manner. If you want pleasant, cheerful residents and promote unity, accentuate the positive.

Here's how the dog poop issue can be presented in a more positive light: *The Board of Directors would like to thank those homeowners who are contributing to the overall appearance of our community by picking up and disposing of their pet's waste in an appropriate manner! If we all do our part to keep our community clean and pet waste free then not only will we be enhancing the curb-appeal of our community but also helping to keep our pets healthy. One of the biggest transmitters of canine diseases is feces. When we pick up after our pets we ensure that we are not contributing to that problem. Thank you again for your thoughtfulness and cooperation!*

See! Isn't that better? If we are going to use words to try to help residents understand the kinds and types of behaviors that are expected of them, we might as well use words that empower and don't intimidate or belittle. It's just as easy to slant an article towards the positive as it is towards the negative. What often happens, however, is that the manager or the board has gotten 'slammed' so hard on some issues that they feel frustrated because they can't solve the problem immediately (remember the value of patience in creating community?). That frustration takes the form of anger and that anger is communicated to the residents through negative newsletter articles. Anger is not a communication tool, it is a weapon.

If the Board or management has gotten into a habit of taking a negative approach in trying to force compliance with association rules, and it doesn't seem to work, the solution may be to try another approach, not get nastier. One of my former employers was fond of saying, "If you always do what you always did, you'll always get what you always got."

Use vendors as a source of information: In some of the associations the most anticipated articles each month are the ones that are submitted by their landscape contractor. People enjoy reading tips on watering, fertilizing, color selection, information on upcoming maintenance projects and other information relevant to the community. Our service contractors are a valuable resource of information about the associations they service. If asked, they should not only provide you with information that you can share with the residents, but they should appreciate the opportunity to contribute to helping make their jobs easier. What works for the board also works for the vendors: If residents understand the things going on within a community, there is going to be more support, understanding and compliance. Vendors need that understanding just as much as the board of directors. Some of the more obvious service vendors to solicit information from are:

- Landscape Service
- Pest Control Service
- Insurance Agent
- Pool Service
- Security Service

If an association is still under developer control, add regular updates from the developer.

Emphasize email addresses in articles: Whenever possible, be sure to include email addresses in the newsletter. It's fairly common for an informational article to end: " . . . and if you have any questions, please contact management." But, it is much more helpful to both the reader and the manager if it is changed to read, " . . . and if you have any questions, please contact our manager, Jane Smith, at Community Association Management Company (555-5555, ext. 000 or by email at; janesmith@email.com). Not only will the owner or resident know who to contact but they will have an option as to how to contact them.

If an association has their own website, and it is functionally equipped with email based forms or email links to management, the newsletter article can direct any questions or concerns to the website. Of all the options, this is the most advantageous to the board because if the website has been designed effectively, the resident can find what they are looking for easily and the communication will automatically go to the correct management team member . . . and the resident can utilize the website 24 hours a day, seven days a week. That is important because it prevents issues or concerns from festering within the mind of the owner should they have the question or concern outside of business hours and have to wait until the office opens before communicating their issue. This kind of 'festering' can cause quite a bit of frustration for the resident when they can't get it off their chest immediately and even more frustration for the manager when they have to field the initial communication and what is really a minor issue has become a major one in the mind of the resident. Providing alternative communication options in the newsletter and directing owners and residents to email and website links goes a long way in reducing time-induced issue frustration and reinforces the perception that the board truly cares about what is going on.

Remember the public relations value of newsletters: Besides being the best source of information, newsletters are one of the best public relations tools available to the board of directors. When I worked for a resort management company, the owner once told me, "if you don't blow your own horn every once in a while, somebody is bound to mistake it for a spittoon." A community association newsletter should contain as much horn blowing as possible.

Given the nature of community associations, the majority of decisions that the board of directors must make, and management must implement, are implemented completely unaware of by the average owner or resident. Sure, there are the very noticeable issues: street slurry projects, assessment increases, re-roofing, etc., but the bulk of issues that a community association deal with on an ongoing basis happen without being noticed. If in the course of a year the board of directors make several dozen very significant and important decisions that positively affect the association and its ability to protect, preserve and enhance the common assets of the association, but they also made one poor choice by awarding the street slurry contract to an inexperienced contractor, and the street slurry project turned into a disaster, then which issues are going to define the perception of the board in the minds of the owners? One very visible disaster or the several dozen 'behind the scenes' successes?

If an association newsletter was published on a regular basis that informed the owners and residents of those successes, then the one disaster wouldn't seem as significant as it does when the owners know nothing about the other successes. Two of the most effective formats to accomplish a little horn blowing are articles in each newsletter that focus on previous board meeting highlights and updates on projects that aim to improve some aspect of the common area.

Board meeting highlights should contain all the regular business decisions that are made, such as approval of previous meeting minutes and acceptance of financial statements, but they should also include brief descriptions of the issues that the board has either made decisions on at the meeting or will need to research for action at an upcoming meeting. Some of the more important issues are certainly deserving of their own separate articles in order to expand upon them and inform owners of their importance and significance to the entire association. Insurance issues, budget preparation, and reserve funding are some of those issues.

Board meeting highlights not only keep owners informed of the type and scope of decisions that the board must face on a regular basis but they also remind them that association business is going on even if they don't see it happening. This is important because that understanding goes a long way in influencing how owners perceive the board and the community association. Hard work on behalf of the entire community is almost always appreciated. Increase the perception that the board is working hard to improve association life and you increase appreciation of that work.

Never assume that just because projects are always going on that the residents understand or even appreciate them. For the most part, residents want to think the best about their community. There is a sense of pride that goes along with home ownership that transcends the boundaries of one's home and extends out into the community-at-large. Keeping residents informed, up-to-date and encouraged about association activities feeds that pride and dismisses some of the negative perceptions that may exist in associations that only communicate with their members when they want money or when a resident has done something wrong and they are in non-compliance with an association rule. If you do not ignore the public relations value of your association newsletter then you will be in a much better position to influence member perceptions about the quality of attention provided by the board of directors and the management company.

Request additional newsletter copies for additional distributions: In the fifteen-plus years that I have been publishing community association newsletters, I can count the number of community associations that have requested additional copies of their newsletters for distribution at board meetings, committee meetings, sales offices, models or to mail to community vendors on one hand. It just isn't something that is given much thought. However, if the newsletter contains all of the elements that we have discussed up to this point, then making them available to residents attending board meetings, committee meetings, potential buyers and vendors makes perfect sense by helping to reinforce the sense of cohesiveness and progress that the board and community is making.

Often times the owners that attend board meetings do so because they have a question that they need answered. Perhaps it is a questions that has been answered in the newsletter but they did not read it (like that would ever happen!). Including a copy of the latest newsletter along with the meeting agenda and distributing them to owners in attendance may answer that question and/or disarm any sense of frustration that the owner may have over the issue.

If committee reports are published in the newsletter then committee chairs should be provided with copies of the newsletter to distribute to their members that may not have brought theirs so that they can discuss the effectiveness of their communication efforts. Committees should be just as sensitive to the communication needs of the owners as the board should be. For many associations, committees are the backbone of the association and their efforts directly impact the decisions made by the board. If the committee report effectively represents the recent efforts of the committee it will not only inform the owners that such a committee even exists in the first place, it may inspire them to volunteer to join it. Contrary to the "Ignorance is Bliss" management style, participation is a good thing—and a necessary condition of creating community!

If the community is new and still being built-out, then the latest newsletter would be a fantastic marketing tool for the sales team. Not only will it allow prospective owners to understand more about association living, but it will underscore their perception that this is a community that cares about its residents and keeps them informed. Besides, as they say, "birds of a feather flock together," so if you position your community as communicative, involved and informed you are more likely to attract new owners who appreciate and embrace those qualities themselves.

Getting service vendors involved in the newsletter is also a great idea. Vendors should not only appreciate being in on the communication loop of the community, but it could increase the quality of service that they provide. Think about it: If I'm the landscaper and know that everyone in the community is being updated on the work that I am doing on a regular basis, I am going to make an extra effort to make that work more attractive. Naturally there are some exceptions, but most vendors take pride in their work and when they feel that their work is appreciated by their clients, they work even harder for them. Positive reinforcement breeds positive results.

Finally, it is a good idea to have your manager carry a few extra issues of the latest newsletter with her during property inspections. Being able to reference it if asked about an issue that had already been addressed or if confronted about a communication issue ("Why should I get involved, the board doesn't really care what I think anyway!") will reinforce the importance of reading the newsletter whenever it is received. As I already alluded to, not everyone reads the association newsletter. Most of the time they assume it is the proverbial "stick" that the board use to keep them in line and don't really care to be told what to do or to be talked "down" to. Whenever there is the opportunity to change that perception and show that the newsletter is a valuable information and communication tool, then take it. Property inspections can provide that opportunity and having an extra newsletter copy handy will allow the manager to make the most of it.

Publish on a regular basis: If you want a newsletter to be effective, it must be published on a regular basis so that the owners and residents learn to expect it. If they don't expect it or it only comes once in a blue moon, then chances are they won't pay any attention to it. That's just one of the facts of life. If owners don't know when to expect a newsletter, they won't be looking for it to arrive. Getting owners and residents in the habit of expecting association information in a regular and timely manner is just as important as the information itself. Remember, we are trying to increase positive perceptions and increasing awareness of when information is forthcoming is a positive thing. Publishing on a regular basis increases that awareness.

A good rule of thumb to follow is that a newsletter should go out as close as possible after the last board of directors meeting. If the board meets monthly, a newsletter should go out monthly. If the board meets bi-monthly, then every other month is sufficient. Not only does this formula work because most often after a board meeting there is more news and information to report, but because the size of the association usually corresponds to the regularity of the board meetings and, let's face it, smaller associations whose boards only meet quarterly don't have as much going on as a larger association that meets monthly.

Also, the expense of a newsletter needs to be taken into account. Unless the management company has the foresight to include communication tools in with their management contract, the smaller associations just don't have the funds available for those tools that a larger association does. It's just a numbers game. It is the financial cost that usually determines how communication tools are utilized. With communication, you don't get what you don't pay for and what you don't get when there is no communication is often times the difference between an association working together to build a stronger community and a collection of homeowners who just tolerate each other and their community association just to get by.

Final Newsletter Comments: I want to end up this section on newsletters by reminding you once again of the comment published in the Community Association Institute's magazine, Common Ground: *"The newsletter is a community association's most valuable communications tool. It is the primary information link with homeowners, the best and most consistent way to keep owners informed of the association's activities."* Information is knowledge and knowledge is empowering. Empowerment creates community.

WEBSITES

There is no better communication, information and document resource tool available that allows for such a profound exchange of two-way information and provide for as many communication options as a community association website. All association forms, documents, rules, policies and procedures can and should be available on any effective community website. In addition, one of the biggest reasons that a community website is so effective is that it allows owners and residents to communicate with the board and management and access community-specific information 24 hours a day/7 days a week. From a community-building perspective providing that option is huge because it empowers the owner to be able to share their comments, concerns and complaints on *their* schedule, not the board's or management's.

As with newsletters, a community website benefits the board's ability to provide a greater quality of service and more effective management. The good news is that an effective website can be accomplished with little more expertise than is needed to use a word processing program. I certainly don't want to argue the advantages or disadvantages of providing professional designed community websites by highly skilled (and expensive) website design professionals. What I do want to do is show you that an effective and extremely user-friendly community website has much more to do with functionality than it does appearance. If the right features are available on the site, then it will do much more for the owners and management than a site that costs thousands of dollars to design and places more emphasis on how it looks than what it does.

Association website fundamentals: The most important element in creating an effective website is to make sure it reflects the needs of the community association and the owners and not the desires of the website designer who probably has little or no experience with community association living or management. You can have the most beautiful site in the world, but if it doesn't do everything that it is capable of, in the community association arena, then not too many people will keep visiting it to take care of their association-related business. Its lack of depth will doom its effectiveness in creating community.

The features of a truly effective website should be based upon several factors, all of which demand that those features represent the real needs of the community. Let's see how we can do that:

Email based forms: The two main goals of any community association website should be to provide communication options and information to the owners and residents. Let's start with providing communication options and discuss email based forms.

Whenever an owner visits the community website, if they can easily find the communication option that best suits the reason they have accessed the site in the first place, then you have already won half the battle. Email based forms create opportunities to address specific communication needs. For example, an owner wants to report a violation of the community's rules and regulations. They go to the community website and there, easily visible on the main menu, is a link to a "Report a Violation" form. The owner clicks on the link and goes to a form that they fill out with all the relevant information and submit. The form is sent to the manager as an email and the manager can then begin to address the non-compliance issue.

Some of the other specific needs that may require email based forms are:

- Request an Architectural Review application
- Request homeowner account information
- Report a common area maintenance issue
- Volunteer to serve on an association committee

- Clubhouse usage application
- Request parking permit applications

I would strongly recommend that a general communication form also be included among the email based forms in order to function as a 'catch-all' in case the particular need of the owner is not addressed by the available forms. Some forms may be eliminated if the specific information being requested by the form is made available on the website in another area, such as Architectural Review Applications, which can be available to download and doesn't have to be directly requested from management via a form.

Direct email links to the management company representatives: It is impossible to address every situation that an owner will need to contact management for with a pre-created form. In addition some people prefer to communicate via email and not through a form. It is for those reasons that there should be several email links available on the community website that go directly to the management company representatives. Depending upon the size and scope of the management company, some links can go to accounting representatives, other to customer service representatives and some to the manager and her assistant.

I can't tell you how many sites I have reviewed that have one email link on them, usually in the "contact us" section of the website. I'm not sure that approach very effectively conveys a very receptive communication policy to the website visitor. Ideally, you want the website visitor to come away from the experience with the perception that the association can hardly wait to hear from them. Email links should be falling from the sky and found everywhere. Every bit of information presented on the site should have an email link preceding it going to the appropriate management company representative in order to invite questions or comments. Chances are most of those email links will not be used, but they sure better be noticed if you want to reinforce a communication-friendly perception among the owners. If you post an online version of your newsletter then you can add an email link after each article for those owners with further questions about the information contained in the article. Announcements, bulletins and breaking community news items should have email links also.

An issue I want to address, but will not spend a lot of time on, is whether to have board or committee member email addresses listed or provide links to them on a community website. I strongly advise against that for two reasons:

1. If you have a manager and/or management company then you are paying them to be the hub of communication for the community association. It is their job to receive all communications directed to the board so that they can be addressed and passed along with appropriate. Bypassing management takes them out of this communication loop and can adversely affect their ability to stay on top of any community issues.

2. Board members are primarily homeowners. They are board members during a board meeting only. One of the reasons many homeowners do not wish to serve on the board is the perception that those duties intrude onto their private lives. If the board allows or encourages direct communication from the community, they are setting a dangerous precedent for future boards and risk losing their homeowner identity completely to other owners. Going for an evening walk, fetching your mail, and even chance encounters in the grocery store take on a whole new experience when other owners only see you as a board member and have an issue to discuss. Can you spell burnout?

Community documents and policies: Besides the communication options that a community website provides, one of the most important roles that any effective site should encompass is that of community information source. Providing access to community documents, policies, information and updates on the website is a highly perceived service by owners and residents. Being able to download the community rules and regulations, the clubhouse rental procedure, assessment collection policy or latest newsletter on the website saves the owner and the manager considerable time.

Using an Adobe Acrobat program, any word processing file can easily be formatted into a PDF file. PDF files have a wide range of advantages:

- **Secure:** Creators of PDF files can prevent the copying of text, editing of text, alteration of graphics, and printing of a document. With PDF format, you can add user-password security at the document level. This enables documents to be sent via email between people or locations without unauthorized viewing of the document.

- **Preserves document integrity:** PDF files retain all of the formatting contained in the original source document. Fonts are embedded in the PDF document, so readers do not need to have the specific fonts used in the document on their computers. Also, all graphics, special characters, and colors display as they were created.

- **Cross-platform:** The PDF format displays a document independently of the hardware, operating system, and application software used to create the original PDF file. It is designed to create transferable documents that can be shared across multiple computer platforms.

- **Readily available:** PDF files can be retrieved, viewed, and printed with the Adobe Acrobat Reader. Anyone, anywhere can open a PDF file if they have the Acrobat Reader software. The Reader is easy to download from the Adobe Web site for free.

- **Speed:** PDF files are compact and often smaller than their source files, allowing PDF files to open quickly. They can be downloaded a page at a time for fast display on the Web and generally do not slow down network systems. A one-page, 8 1/2 x 11 document is often about 1,000 kilobytes in size, but, when converted into PDF format, can compress to approximately 25-35 kilobytes.

- **Distribute anywhere:** PDF files can be published and distributed anywhere, including in print, attached to an email, on corporate servers, posted on Web sites, or on a CD-ROM. PDF files display as created, regardless of installed fonts, software, and operating systems. When you print a PDF file it looks the same way it displays and it prints correctly on almost any printing device.

As mentioned earlier, many community forms, such as Architectural Review Applications, can easily be made available for owners to download, print, complete and mail into management. Email based forms are not the best format to use for forms that require additional material to be sent in along with the form or application. For example, an Architectural Review Application will probably need to have proposed plans or blueprints submitted along with the form. Most owners won't have those plans or blueprints available in a digital format to send along with the form/application so they will have to be sent via regular mail. It could cause an administrative challenge for the management company to have all the required information being sent separately and by different mediums. The easiest solution is to provide the architectural review application for downloading on the community website and require that it, along with any accompanying plans or fees, be mailed in or delivered to the management company. That way it eliminates any possible confusion or lost information. Sometimes the easiest solution is not the most technologically advanced solution.

Some of the documents the board should consider providing on a community website are:

1. Architectural Review Forms
2. Parking Permit Forms
3. Insurance Disclosure Documents
4. Current Fiscal Year Budget
5. Clubhouse Rental Forms
6. Parking Regulations
7. Pool & Spa Rules
8. Approved Board Meeting Minutes
9. Upcoming Board Meeting Agenda Items
10. Latest Newsletter
11. Color or Design Specifications
12. CC&Rs/By-Laws

Increasing the perceived value of the community website: I've mentioned perceived value before, I want to define it further for you. When anyone uses a service or product, that service or product is perceived by the user as having a certain value. Sometimes that value is high. Sometimes that value is low. Take a hotel room, for example. If you check into your room and the hotel does not have any room service, mini-bar, or laundry service, just hotel room basics: bed, phone, TV, sink shower and linen. The perceived value of that hotel by the guest is undoubtedly fairly low. However, if that room only costs $50 per night to stay in, then the perceived value increases as those additional amenities would only cause the cost of the room to go up and the guest's perception might reflect a greater importance on saving money than on amenities. This type of perceived values is dependent entirely upon the state of mind of the guest and the quality of the actual services or product is secondary.

The problem with this kind of approach is that it is extremely difficult, if not impossible, to control the state of mind of any number of possible guests. Some guests will be happy and have a perceived high value of their—because it saves them money—while others will be unhappy and have a low perceived value of their room, because they expect more amenities. You can mitigate the unhappy guests by extensively marketing your hotel as a budget, economy, no-frills destination, but by doing so you reduce your potential guest market considerably. The guests who come back will only be the ones who want to save money, all others will stay away.

Since we can't control anyone's state of mind, we have to relegate any successful efforts at increasing perceived value to expanding the product, in this case the room and amenities, so that it offers more—in order to increase the perceived value to those guests who expect more than just a room, toilet and television—but keeps the costs down—in order to maintain the perceived value of return guests who appreciate the economical rates. By adding inexpensive amenities, such as coffee makers, mini-bars, free newspapers, overnight laundry service and even room service through arrangements with a neighboring restaurant, you increase the perceived value of the room for everyone.

Now, let's take this example and apply it to a community website. The website can provide strictly community-specific information: email links, forms, documents, and community news. Owners who visit the site can take care of association-related business, but that's it. Many board members are content with this type of community website because it sticks to the business of the community association, period. Those homeowners who value their association site in terms of supplying the rules & regulations, required forms, governing documents and common area maintenance reporting, will be content also. Even managers who have learned to view their work by the letter of the law (and contract) and limit their perceptions about the nature of community associations will be satisfied with a strictly 'business-only' community website. The perceived value of the community website will be high among those elements of the community association. Any owners/board members/ managers who have a more expansive perception of their community association will probably not view this community website with a very high degree of perceived value.

The legal purpose of the community association is to protect, preserve and enhance the assets of the association. That, in essence, is the letter of the law. The happiness, sense of community belonging, or neighborliness of the community members are not the responsibility of the community association, according to the letter of the law. Even the types and kind of communication we have been discussing fall outside of the legal responsibilities of the association and the management company. However, as I've tried to demonstrate, accomplishing the goals of the letter of the law can really only be achieved successfully by embracing those elements that demonstrate the spirit of community association living: community unity, harmony, a sense of belonging, neighborliness, and a feeling that one's life is better by living in the community. The vision of the community association for leaders that embrace the spirit of community association living and those who embrace the 'no-frills/business only' approach, differs not just in depth but also in effectiveness. Which community associations are better equipped to protect, preserve and enhance the common assets of the association? The ones that limits their vision to the letter of the law or the ones who realize that the letter of the law is best complied with by embracing and supporting the spirit of community association living and all the peripherals that help create community-consciousness?

There's a quote in A Course In Miracles that best exemplifies the possibilities that exist when we work at bringing together individual homeowners to create a sense of community:

Alone we can do nothing,
But together our minds fuse into something
Whose power is far beyond
The power of its separate parts.

So, let's add some 'spirit' to the community website in order to foster those elements that contribute to the 'letter' of the association's purpose. In doing so, just as in the example of the hotel room, we can increase the perceived value of the community website. Here are some examples of community website features that address a broader vision of the association:

- Association social events calendar
- Online community bulletin board
- Local civic events calendar
- Links to other local businesses
- Local traffic information links
- Driving directions to anywhere
- Current weather conditions and forecasts
- Recreational activity information for the area
- First Aid & emergency help information
- Local restaurant guides and reviews
- Online telephone white & yellow pages
- Parents resource guide & community babysitting directory
- Online community classified ads

Don't Be Afraid To Brainstorm!

The kinds and types of non association-business related features are limited only by the imagination of the association leaders. You would be surprised how many website features you can come up with during a 15-minute brainstorming session between the board of directors. The main point here to remember is that every community association member has many roles in their life. Being a member of their community association is only one of them. It is advantageous to the goals of the community association, whether it is through the newsletter or community website, to recognize those other roles in order to create more positive interest and participation in the association. Increasing the perceived value of the community website, by adding non association-business related features, attempts to address that recognition.

Marketing your community website: Even if you build it, they still may not come. If no one in the community knows about the community website then it is not going to be utilized very often and management won't benefit from any of the time management advantages it provides. Of the over a hundred and fifty different community association websites that we have designed and maintained in the past decade, there is a definite correlation between website traffic and newsletter production. In other words, those associations that have regular newsletters also have the most traffic on their community websites. Those associations that do not have a newsletter, or publish it infrequently, have noticeably low levels of website traffic.

As I have stated already, a community website and a regularly published newsletter are both required elements in an effective proactive community association communication policy. The newsletter compliments the website and visa versa. But what is equally important is the marketing opportunities that the newsletter provides when it comes to getting the word out about the community website to members and residents. When I talk about 'marketing' the website I intend it to have the same connotations that would apply to marketing any product or service. Merriam-Webster defines marketing to mean "the process or technique of promoting, selling, and distributing a product or service." When discussing community websites, the newsletter is the most effective tool to promote the site, sell it's advantages and distribute its location (URL Address).

If I remember correctly, there are certain maxims of marketing and advertising that relate to guiding people's behaviors in a certain direction in order to obtain a desired result. One of these is that the average person needs to 'see' an advertisement at least seven times before they internalize the ad enough to develop a desire for whatever the ad is promoting. Effective marketing means getting the word out over, and over, and over again, before any change in consumer behavior occurs. Marketing a community website is no different than marketing soap. Before an owner is likely to internalize the benefits and opportunities that their community website will provide them, they have to be told about it repeatedly. Just as before any consumer is likely to buy a certain brand of soap, they are going to have to be convinced that the certain product meets their needs better than the other brands of soap available, owners have to be convinced that their community association experience can be greatly enhanced through the use of their community website. That convincing can only be achieved through repeated exposure to the product, or in our case, the community website. That's what a regularly published association newsletter can do. Here's how:

- Whenever owners or residents are asked to contact management, list the community website address in addition to phone numbers and email addresses.
- An informational article about the community website should be in every issue that lists some of its features and advantages.
- List the community website address in all important numbers or contact areas of the newsletter.

- At the top or bottom of every newsletter page, note the community website address.
- If a newsletter is sent out on a regular basis, doing those things will increase the owners/residents awareness of their community website. If they know it is there, there is a much better chance that they will visit it. It may just take some time to get them to know it's there, so be patient and be persistent.

Getting The Word Out

The newsletter, although the most effective marketing tool, is not the only way to get the word out about a community website. Here are some other suggestions:

- Have the community website address printed on all letterhead and correspondence going out from the community association.

- Print the website address on monthly billing statements or payment reminder notices that go out to owners. Associations that use coupon books to pay their assessments should have the website address printed on them.

- List the community website on any bulletins or handouts (such as meeting agendas at the board meetings) that are given to owners.

- If there is a voice mail box dedicated to the association, be sure to announce the site address.

- Whenever communicating with an owner or resident, be sure to mention the community website. If it is via email, list the website address at the end of the email. Always encourage use of the website as an alternative communication option.

- Have index cards that fit in a Rolodex made up for the members of the association that list important management company contact information (including the website address).

- At the Annual Meeting, add an agenda item that allows a member of the website committee or management representative to discuss the advantages of using the community website and provide an appropriate handout that attendees can take home and post on their refrigerator, computer, etc.

- Encourage word-of-mouth promotion among owners and residents. Remind board and committee members to get in the habit of discussing the site with their neighbors.

- Register the community website on popular search engines (i.e., Google, Yahoo). Many search engines have an "Add Your Site" option to their main marketing menu. This will help identify your site if someone doesn't know the address and searches for it on the internet. There are firms out there that will do this for you and list the site on all major search engines, however this service is fee-based.

Creating a community website and making sure that it has all the features necessary in order to achieve our goal of helping to create community is only the first step. Making sure the owners and residents know about the website is the most important step. If no one knows about the site, no one is going to visit it. It doesn't get any simpler than that!

Social Networking

As I mentioned before, the popularity of Facebook is creating another opportunity to reach out to owners. Besides the sense of belonging that it creates, social networking sites can help to redefine the perceptions of just what it is that the community association is all about. Consider this: Just as adding website content that is not community association related helps to increase the perceived value of that website, participating in social networking sites helps to increase the perceived value of the community association itself. Here's how. With over 500 million users, Facebook has added a new dimension to connecting with others. It has very quickly become part of our social fabric and those people who are members of Facebook value the connections that they have with others on the site. Being on Facebook is considered a positive element of their lives. Companies, organizations, clubs and other groups have quickly embraced social networking as a way to reach out to others, establish a base of connection and inform others about their activities and/or products. Because Facebook is considered a positive force in people's lives, at this time, most of those who also are on Facebook are perceived of as being positive opportunities to connect, become informed, educated and stay in touch.

Community associations should also embrace the opportunities that social networking provides. Not only would establishing a Facebook presence (for example) be advantageous in helping owners within the community connect and stay informed, but just because of its affiliation with Facebook, the perception of the community can be re-shifted and instead of being thought of with indifference or scorn, can be consciously redefined to be embraced as a 'friend.' Having a Facebook presence allows for greater opportunities to unite others while changing perceptions. There are some guidelines that I will recommend in a moment that should be kept in mind, but for the most part, boards of directors should seriously consider the advantages of establishing a social networking presence in order to further their community building efforts.

Cautionary Note

Before I discuss how the best ways to utilize social networking sites, there are some potential challenges that must be addressed. When I suggest that a Facebook presence would be beneficial to any board's community building efforts, I am not implying that community associations need to embrace all of the interactive dialogue features of Facebook and other social networking sites . . . at least not at the beginning of the community building process. Until there is a noticeable improvement in community participation and involvement in creating community, giving owners an opportunity to post their thoughts, concerns, complaints, judgments and predictions for everyone to read on the community site can easily create more divisiveness within the community and sabotage any community building efforts. No one, community associations aside, want their dirty laundry—real or perceived—hanging out there for everyone to see and comment on. Becoming tall by cutting off the heads of others is an attitude that seems pervasive in our culture and if you look at many social network site posts, there is a lot of whining and finger-pointing going on. Whatever is wrong with one's life tends to be the result of being 'wronged' by someone or some thing and posting that 'wrong' has become a sort of therapy for many. Can you imagine the ruckus that one owner can create if they post a comment that is critical of the board and is based on false rumors? The domino effect could easily unhinge any advances the board has achieved in uniting community members.

I've not heard or seen of any successful attempts at giving owners or residents a public and unbridled vehicle for sharing their perceptions about their community and their community leaders with their neighbors. Unsupervised blogs, bulletin board posts, the ability to send universal emails throughout the community, just don't reinforce the positive perceptions that are needed in order to create community because many people use those forums to unload their frustrations with. These negative posts tend to unite neighbors, but they become united for all the wrong reasons. It is easy to find fault with any community association management if one looks close enough, what is difficult is coming up with workable solutions to community challenges. Negative posts seldom do anything more than point fingers and fail to provide any real solutions other than 'get rid of the bums.'

When we talk about empowering owners, about encouraging them to identify problems, suggest solutions and implement those solutions, we are talking about doing so in a structured, positive-oriented environment. Not in an environment that is prone to tearing down as opposed to building up. We can embrace the benefits of changing perceptions about the community that social networking sites provide without having to embrace all of the features that those sites provide. It is much better for the board to just use the site as another communication tool to provide owners with community news and information about community meetings, activities, events and projects—without allowing input from owners regarding that information. When owners join or 'friend' the community site, all information posted by the board will be pushed to their friend's 'wall' and if the owner has email notification enabled, the information will also be sent to their email address. What board would not want that ability in pursuit of their community building efforts? Again, another no-brainer.

To accomplish the task of establishing a social network presence, consider the following:

- Establish an ad-hoc committee that would be responsible for collecting information and posting it on the site
- When establishing the site, do so as an organization and disable the ability to comment on posts
- Make sure the feature that allows all information posted on the site to be posted on friend's walls is enabled
- Tell owners about the site via the newsletter and community association website on a regular basis and invite them to join

- Encourage owners to tell their neighbors about the site and join it
- Post information on a regular basis even if it is redundant
- Post links to the community association website and manager's email address on the site
- Whenever anything is added to the community website, such as latest approved minutes, upcoming meeting agendas, maintenance project updates, forms, etc., announce it on a post to the social networking site and provide a link to that information/document
- Consider holding online town hall meetings on the social networking site at which time the ability to comment can be enabled for a specified period of time and, using a moderator, allow registered owners to comment on community issues

CONCLUSION

The effective use of all the communication tools by the board of directors demands persistence, flexibility and dedication. Every community is unique, not just in the demographics of who reside within it, but in its history, its challenges and its strengths. Using a newsletter, website or social networking site and accentuating the positives, inviting participation and taking action based upon community input is an ongoing process that has no end. It can always get better. At times all communities take a step back, the key is to take two steps forward when that happens. As leadership within the community evolves and changes, it is important to remember that the effective use of the communication tools must remain constant. Without communication none of the elements of creating community can be established.

COMMITTEE WORK

The Legs of Empowerment

"Alone we can do so little; together we can do so much."
—Helen Keller

I expect that the response to everything presented so far is probably, "So, all is well and good in theory, but how do I really get others to buy into the concept of an enhanced sense of community? How do I get volunteers to join committees so that we can implement these ideas?" Community consciousness can act like a magnet. If you embrace it, practice the strategies and techniques presented and do so with positive enthusiasm and focus, others will join you simply because of the power of your commitment. One person, acting virtuously (making the right choices, at the right time, for the right reasons) is all that is needed in order to begin the journey of creating community. When others take notice, are invited to join in and choose to contribute their time and energy to creating community it is essential that there is a place for them at the table, so to speak. There has to be well-defined goals established for them to accomplish. Those goals and the tasks needed to accomplish them are taken up by the work of committees. Without committees there can be no real empowerment within the structure of a community association.

In my experience of working with dysfunctional community associations, one of the most common sentiments expressed by their boards of directors regarding committees are usually sentiments of either frustration or control. Frustration because they can't seem to find anyone willing to serve on committees, and control because they want to keep an eye on the committees to ensure that are not working in opposition to what the board wants—or in the case of a community that has been hijacked by Lou Sifer—in opposition to what the self-serving, ego-maniacal, know-it-all president of the board wants. The first challenge (frustration) can be eased by the techniques and strategies already discussed. The second challenge probably ensures that none of the same strategies or techniques will ever be practiced or implemented in the first place. We will briefly discuss escaping from community association hijackers later. Now, let's look into the nature of committee work and how to utilize them in such a manner that volunteering to serve on them becomes a privilege and attracts owners with a minimum amount of effort.

Just as the creation of community happens in stages, so should the development of committees. One of the big mistakes that many boards make is to create a number of committees and populate them with board members or their significant others. The goal is not to create a committee just for the sake of having a committee and then add the most convenient members just to have members. The goal is to provide an effective means for owners, who have up until now, avoided participation in community affairs in order to empower them and expand the boundaries of their community role.

When we look at the reason that many owners volunteer to serve on committees, we see that sometimes their motivation is linked to being angry at some perceived wrong perpetuated by the board or association, and a self-serving desire to change that perceived wrong. For example, Lou Sifer gets fed up with what he perceives as a lack of community security and launches an attack on the board of directors, management and the security company. His sense of boundaries regarding the security of his home was violated and regardless of the true cause, he chose to be angry, react negatively and refuse to acknowledge responsibility for the cause of the boundary violation. From a psychological perspective, anger is important because it helps us establish boundaries. Whenever our boundaries are crossed, we feel violated and we respond by getting angry. We then internalize that sense of boundary and avoid circumstances and environments that may pose a risk of violating that boundary in order to avoid falling into anger. The secret to transforming anger from a destructive affect to a constructive choice—and help create community—is to help owners expand their sense of community boundaries. Their boundaries have to exist beyond the walls of their home and extend out to include their neighbors, the common areas they share with their neighbors and the conduct exhibited by everyone who lives within or visits the community. In addition, those boundaries have to be flexible in order to accommodate the wide range of personalities that live within the community. To expand boundaries that become rigid only creates more opportunities for feeling anger. Flexible boundaries allow for change and growth and adaptation, all necessary components of living well with others.

How do we expand our psychological boundaries from the limited experiences that take place within our home to include the common experiences of community association living? By promoting inclusion and providing positive opportunities for owners to reduce the rigidity of their current sense of boundary and test the waters of a more expansive sense of belonging through committee work. If the board of directors of the community association in which Lou Sifer lived had embraced some of the principles of creating community, then when Lou blew a gasket about the burglary of his home, instead of dismissing his rants, they would have invited him to help solve his perceived boundary violation by joining or chairing a security committee. Then, instead of soliciting his neighbors to join his campaign to overthrow the current board of directors, he could have used his energy to understand more about the security issues of the community, invited those neighbors to join him on the committee and made a positive contribution to his community instead of trying to tear it down and rebuild it in his image. The board could have empowered Lou instead of covering him up.

Whether it is security or parking or barking dogs or architectural controls, there are bound to be community issues that push the buttons and threaten the comfortable boundaries of nearly every owner. Some owners choose to have flexible boundaries in order to avoid feeling violated and some owners have rigid boundaries and choose to exist in a continual state of anger. Anger creates adrenalin in the body and adrenalin addiction is a very real problem in the world and impacts everyone that the adrenalin junkie comes in contact with, but for the purposes of this book, we are going to ignore adrenalin rehab as a viable course of action in creating community—although it has its merits. Instead, we are going to look at providing alternative methods of venting anger and frustration that can be harnessed for the greater good of the community association: Committee work.

Committee Fundamentals

The obvious advantages of utilizing committees include:

- It can spread the work to be done among a number of people,
- More ideas about an issue are generated when more people are involved,
- Members feel better about an organization when they are involved in running it,
- People are more willing to work on something when they have taken part in planning it.

The first rule of forming a committee is, keep it small. The bigger the committee the harder it will be to arrange meetings and reach a decision, so restrict the size to the minimum possible.

The board of director's power to form committees is usually addressed in the community association's bylaws. A typical bylaw provision on this subject usually allows the board to form any type of committee it deems appropriate, and also allows the board to delegate certain powers to a committee. It's important to note that although a board can delegate certain powers to a committee, it's the board of directors that's ultimately responsible for the decisions it makes based on the work of a committee.

When committees are formed: Standing committees are generally formed at the onset of an organization's existence—usually at the first or second meeting of a newly formed board (i.e., landscape, rules, finanical, parking, social, newsletter committees). Special committees (ad hoc committees), on the other hand, usually evolve from a board discussion of a pressing matter or issue that needs attention. At this time, the board asks volunteer owners or other directors to sit on the committee in order to study the issue and make a recommendation to the full board. The formation of an ad hoc committee is noted in the minutes of the board meeting, along with what the committee's mission is, who will serve on it, who will chair it, and what time frame it is on to accomplish its mission. Once the mission of the ad hoc committee has been accomplished, the committee is disbanded.

Who sits on a committee: In standing committees that require special expertise, the function of a committee drives who will serve on it. The board of directors looks at its roster and decides who would fulfill the functions of a particular. An organization's financial committee generally requires that at least one committee member be well-versed in financial matters. Where a committee is formed to accomplish a specific task, special expertise may not be as important as other considerations, such as which committee members have the time to devote themselves to the task.

What a committee's process looks like: After a committee is appointed, it usually schedules its own meetings. The first point of order at an initial committee meeting is to decide what the scope of the task is, what form the committee's work product will take (for example, a report, a recommendation, an evaluation, and so on), and who will do what to accomplish the committee's goal. Minutes of committee meetings may be taken, depending on the formality of the meetings, the type of committee, and the tasks assigned. However, where a committee needs to report to the board on a periodic or ongoing basis, minutes are usually required. When a committee concludes its task, the committee chair reports the findings and recommendations to the full board of directors. Discussion of the committee's conclusion generally follows, and individual committee members may supplement the conclusion and answer questions from the board at large. If the committee's conclusion requires some form of action from the board, a vote usually follows the committee's report and is made part of the board minutes. (*)

Stages of Committee Formation

A Clear Purpose: As just mentioned, many of the committees, or the power to form committees and their scope, are spelled out in the association bylaws. However, every committee should have a detailed 'map' of its goals, objectives and mission, its limitations and course of action. Nothing ruins a committee's efforts like the lack of a meaningful, clearly stated purpose. Without a clearly stated, reasonable set of goals, the committee will not have the focus it needs to be successful. This map is called a charter and should be created and revisited as necessary in order to ensure that it remains relevant. Once established, the committee charter needs to be formally adopted by the board of directors and its approval noted in the board meeting minutes. Following is an example of an established charter for a landscape committee for Sunshine Acres Community Association (SACA):

SUNSHINE ACRES COMMUNITY ASSOCIATION
LANDSCAPE COMMITTEE CHARTER

WHEREAS, several members of the Sunshine Acres Community Association have expressed a desire to serve on a landscape committee for the community.

WHEREAS, the Board of Directors believes that it is in the Association's best interest to utilize the efforts of these volunteer members to assist Management in reviewing the large amount of common area within the community and provide monthly reports to the Board of Directors.

IT IS THEREFORE RESOLVED, that the Board of Directors of the Association hereby establishes the Sunshine Acres Community Association Landscape Committee (SALC) pursuant to this Charter as follows:

1. **Purpose.** The purpose of the SALC shall be to inspect the common areas within the Association and report landscape maintenance issues to Committee Chair for review and then forwarded to Management for review and consideration by the Board of Directors.
2. **Number of Members**. The SALC should have no less than one (1) member from each neighborhood.
3. **Appointment/Removal of Members.** Only one (1) Board Member must serve on the SALC as a Board Representative. At least one Board member must serve on the SALC as a Board Representative. Members of the SALC serve at the discretion of the Board of Directors and may be removed from the SALC by a majority vote of the Board of Directors.
4. **Appointment of Chairman:** The Board of Directors shall appoint one member to serve as Chairman of the SALC by majority vote of the Board of Directors. The Committee

Chairman serves at the discretion of the Board of Directors and may be removed from the SALC by a majority vote of the Board of Directors.

5. **Meetings.** The SALC shall walk their assigned areas on their own once per month and then report their findings to the Committee Chairman. The Committee Chair can call voluntary meetings to discuss committee concerns amongst its members. Only the Committee Chair is to be invited to attend the monthly landscape walks with Management, the appointed Board Representative and the Association's landscape contractor. During this monthly landscape walk, Management shall be responsible for preparing a punch list to be reviewed by the Board of Directors. Aside from Management's punch list, the Chairman will be responsible for compiling the notes and/or highlights from all its members for the Board of Directors to review at the meeting.

6. **Reports.** The Chairman (or other designated representative in his absence) shall report to the Board of Directors at the monthly meetings as to the progress and status of ongoing maintenance issues as noted by the SALC.

7. **Authorization.** The SALC shall have no authority to direct the Association's landscape maintenance company or Association vendors to take any action. Only the Board of Directors or Management, at the direction of the Board of Directors, may direct the landscape maintenance company to act on behalf of the Association. Any communications received from homeowners to the SALC shall be forwarded to Management for review by the Board of Directors. Upon resolution by the Board of Directors, Management will respond to the individual homeowner and notify the SALC of the outcome. The SALC shall have no authority to spend any amount of money for the Association. Instead, the SALC Chairman shall report their

cumulative recommendation to the Board of Directors for consideration.

8. **Amendment/Revocation.** This SALC Charter may be amended by the Board of Directors at any time.

9. **Association Documentation.** Management shall provide the SALC with copies of available landscape maps, landscape budget information, monthly landscape work order summaries and Board of Directors approvals via the monthly meeting minutes.

* A member of the Committee can only be a homeowner of the Association.

A well informed leader: The leader of a committee must realize that the success or failure of that committee rests squarely on her shoulders. The primary duty of the leader is to guide the group's discussions. She should encourage every member to participate in the meetings and keep the discussion focused on the matter at hand. Meetings should start and end as scheduled and an agenda should be established and followed. The leader is also responsible for encouraging opportunities for interactions between the members and committee members should be provided the opportunity to get to know each other. Groups tend to work better if the members are familiar with one another. If members don't get along well, the leader must not allow those members to impede the flow of the meeting. A quick solution is not to allow the conflicting people to sit near each other or in the direct line of fire.

Dedicated members: In theory, committee members should be carefully selected. These are the people who will help resolve issues for the entire community association. They should be somewhat knowledgeable in the area of the committee's responsibility. Committee members should be a diverse group without being incompatible. Try to recruit people with different perspectives. Remind members that they should be receptive and open to new ideas and other people's opinions as work is accomplished in a committee through the give and take of an open, uninhibited discussion.

In practice, most community associations can seldom afford the luxury of turning down offers of help from their owners, regardless of their lack of experience or knowledge, and should encourage each and every owner to consider volunteering for an association committee that interests them. Strong committee chairs who are familiar with the dynamics of successful committee work (more on that later) are essential in promoting the kind of dynamic within the committee that builds dedication. As the community building effort advances and more owners choose to become involved, the board or committee chair can begin to be more discriminating regarding owners to serve on the committees. At the onset though, embrace everyone who express an interest in committee work.

Some qualities to look for and encourage in all prospective members of any committee are:

- a personal interest in the committee's central issues
- a positive attitude and enthusiasm
- a willingness to communicate
- an ability to work with others

Duties of committee members:
—The **chairperson** conducts all meetings of the committee, maintaining order and supervising all voting within the committee. The chairperson has to have qualities of leadership, patience, diplomacy and public speaking ability. If the committee has to make a statement it will come from the chairperson.

—The **vice-chairperson** has no specific duties other than standing in for the chairperson when he or she is unable to be present. Often this year's vice-chairperson is next year's chairperson in waiting.

—The **secretary** takes notes of all meetings and distributes a copy of these notes to all committee members within a reasonable amount of time after the meeting. Secretaries often assist the chairperson when work is required outside of committee meetings. The ideal Secretary is well organized, has a good knowledge of computers including word processing and graphics programs, and is a good communicator. Often, the chairperson functions in the secretary role, especially when the number of members prohibits having more than one member in a leadership role.

—The **treasurer** prepares and keeps all the committee's financial records. It's a role that demands honesty and fiscal accuracy. Many community association committees do not need a treasurer unless the committee is given a specific budget (such as a social committee).

A Committee is a team-building experience. It is the underlying structure of most groups in society and reflects the basic principles of democracy. **Committees are an integral part of every successful organization and a committee with a clear purpose, a well-informed leader and dedicated members is on its way toward success.**

Attributes of a Strong Committee Chair
Many owners will be new to the committee process. Therefore the committee chair must model the behavior expected of members. A chair helps to frame the issues and sets the tone for the committee's discussions. At the first meeting, which is vitally important to the entire process, a chair sets expectations about the contributions expected from committee members. A chair who is committed and serious will elicit similar levels of commitment and seriousness from the committee.

The responsibility that a chair brings to the work of the committee will determine how the rest of the committee approaches the task. The aim should be an ambitious one: to include and hear the contributions of the other committee members and decide upon recommendations to the board the reflect that listening and those contributions.

At the first meeting the chair must guide the committee to agree on a work plan and, if possible, on how their recommendations will be reported to the board. But first the chair must ensure that the committee clearly understands why it was constituted, its charge, and what is expected of it by the board of directors and the community. This discussion should not be shortchanged. Members will bring to the study personal interests that extend beyond the charge to the committee and may desire to reframe the issues. If the committee chair does not sit on the board, is important to invite board members to talk with the committee at its first meeting and to spend as much time as necessary ensuring that the focus and boundaries of the committee's purpose are well understood. If the committee considers it essential to modify its purpose, it can do so only with the formal approval of the board of directors.

The chair must encourage the expression and constructive discussion of diverse viewpoints. At every meeting, each committee member should feel that he or she has had a full opportunity to express opinions and otherwise contribute to the committee process.

The chair must keep the committee members actively engaged. Volunteers must always feel that their time is being used productively, which requires careful planning of each meeting agenda and of individual committee member assignments—if any—between meetings by the chair. The first meeting should set the example. All members should be encouraged to express their own viewpoints on the focus of the committee and the reason for their involvement. First-time committee members may incorrectly assume that they have the same concerns that everyone else on the committee has. Thus, while it is important for members to express their individual goals, it is also crucial for them to understand that their goals and viewpoints may not be the same as those of the committee in general and may sometimes be in opposition to the committee's formal recommendations to the board. It is important, at the beginning, for all committee members to agree to disagree at times. Committees have a diverse composition—this both adds to its strength and complicates the process of reaching consensus. The chair therefore must always be concerned with the committee's progress toward consensus. Fairness and flexibility are required to move beyond initial differences that sometimes can be considerable, to achieving a group consensus that goes well beyond the obvious, and yet move the issues forward. However, when consensus is not possible or if reaching consensus would skew an important majority position of the committee, it is better to expose the lack of consensus than to obscure it completely through compromise.

Even though there may be some disagreement about part (or all) of the committees recommendations, when making those recommendations to the board, the chair should ensure that the entire committee takes full ownership of the report that it has produced and signs off on the report's findings, conclusions, and recommendations. This is much easier if most committee members—regardless of their personal viewpoints—have contributed and engaged in the process of reviewing and revising the initial recommendations. At this stage it is also extremely important the committee understands the nature of the board's review process of their recommendations. Not all committee recommendations will or should be accepted carte blanche. Committees are sometimes unprepared to have their work criticized when reviewed by the board. Under these circumstances, they may resent the fact that the review may produce demands for significant changes to their initial recommendations. The chair should remind the committee of this step throughout the deliberative process—particularly if the committee begins to endorse recommendations that are not based strongly on evidence. For example, a safety committee may make a recommendation to the board that speed bumps be installed throughout the community, even though there has been no significant history of speeding within the community, in order to act as a deterrent to speeding in the future.

The plan for the first committee meeting: When committee members assemble for the first time, they are likely to have many questions, such as:
- What is the committee really about?
- What is the plan for making recommendations?
- Who are my colleagues on the committee?
- What can I contribute?
- What is the role of the committee and the board?

The answers to these questions create impressions that will influence the committee's work. Thus, it is very important for the first meeting to be well planned and conducted.

The objectives of the first meeting almost always include the following:

- To introduce the committee to its responsibilities by clearly conveying the committee's charter
- To describe the expectations for the committees work by the board of directors
- To identify issues that may be potentially controversial or contentious
- To explain the committee process, including the recommendation review under which the recommendations will be conducted by the board of directors

- To discuss and adopt a work plan for the committee that encompasses such elements as inspection methods, committee assignments, topics for future meetings, and so on
- To allow committee members to get better acquainted and begin the process of building trust among them

Meeting management: Much must be accomplished in the limited time the committee is together. In planning a committee meeting, chairs should keep certain considerations in mind:

- Every meeting should have clear objectives derived from the committee's charter and mission and from the progress of the work completed to date.
- Each meeting's agenda should be designed to support that meeting's objectives and should state those objectives clearly.
- The meeting agenda should be lean and flexible since meetings often run short on time.
- All committee meetings should include anyone in the community who wishes to attend but does not wish to join the committee in order to create a greater understanding of the committee and influence their decision to join it at a later date.
- —Periodic breaks and committee socials should be scheduled to pace the committee's work and to promote effective working relations among the members and the board.

Many preparations are needed as a meeting is planned:

- If community business partners are asked to address the committee, requests to the partner should be made in writing. These requests should clearly indicate what the committee would like to know and the context for the information being sought, as well as the time that will be allotted for this purpose.

- Committee members should be sent reading materials for the meeting far enough in advance that they can be well prepared.
- The chair should be fully conversant with the meeting agenda and overall work plan.

Effective chairs have developed many ideas for managing meetings successfully:

- Be clear that all members are expected to be present for the entire meeting.
- Make sure that each speaker is aware of the time constraints on his or her comments to the committee. Be strict in pushing along speakers who are taking too much time.
- Watch for members who are holding back their opinions and draw them into the meeting.
- Be quick to bring straying discussions back to the focus of the meeting.
- At the end of the meeting, note what was accomplished, what remains to be done, and what subsequent actions are to be taken by the committee.

Final tips for committee chairs:

- The success of a committee depends a great deal on how well it is put together in the beginning, even before the committee has its first meeting. And if the chair can be brought into that process at any stage, it's a very good thing
- Every chair should consider writing a brief letter to committee members outlining his or her view of the charge, providing some context-setting statements, and offering some guidance (both "do's and don'ts") to prepare for the first meeting and think about the committee's unique role—i.e., about what it is going to do that no one else had done before

- Other owner contribution is often very large. They add a great deal to the definition and expression of ideas. They are very much a part of the team even if not a part of the committee.
- The first meeting is to, first of all, get the committee members to know each other and their backgrounds so that one can understand the basis from which the members move into discussion.
- Write down the conclusions and recommendations that come from those conclusions. Formulating conclusions and recommendations means you have gone through the intellectual rigor of discussion, debate, and deliberations and come to consensus in terms of which direction the committee wants to go regarding their recommendations.
- Consensus may mean that there are different points of view. Very often the differences relate to value systems rather than to fact or relationships. These can be recognized and stated in a way that all members recognize as fair and balanced. It's very important for the chair and committee to recognize that it can achieve consensus as to what the issues are and what the different views on those issues are without necessarily coming to complete agreement.
- The board's review process has the potential to dramatically improve the initial recommendation.
- New chairs ought to know that it can be fun and that it is extraordinarily educational even as it is challenging. There are very positive rewards and good feelings afterwards.

Empowering Others Through Committee Work

When we revisit the stages of empowerment, all three of them (Find out what people are thinking and what they believe the problems are; Let them design the solutions, and; Get out of the way and let them put those solutions into practice) are best accomplished through the effective use of the committee paradigm within a community association's culture of community building. If communication is the best tool to use in creating community, committees are the vehicle that get us there.

Board members should always be on the lookout for prospective committee members. That means that when approached while walking their dog, picking up their mail or just walking in the neighborhood by an owner who has a community concern they should invite them to consider either joining or helping create a committee to look into the matter. I've worked with numerous board presidents who refuse to accept the possibility of forming new committees based upon need. They remain stuck in their determination to keep the committees to a minimum and based entirely upon those designated in the bylaws (and some even ignore those). It's the age-old "too many chefs spoil the soup" style of leadership that they believe worked for them when they ran Spacely Sprocketts or lead their current 'for profit' business venture with. The problem with that style of leadership is that it is really a form of dictatorship—that many privately held businesses embrace—by reducing the input that is provided by those being led. We've already determined that such a style does not work in creating community.

Let's do an exercise in helping us recognize the kinds of committees that your specific community association might be able to benefit from.

Exercise: Make a list of all the issues within your community that can be considered a 'problem.' What rules are the board continually being challenged with in order to gain compliance with the association's governing documents or rules and regulations? What topics are most frequently brought to the board's attention during the open forum sessions of the board meeting? Now, next to each issue/rule compliance challenge identify what kind of committee can be created in order to deal with that issue/challenge.

You will probably have a much longer list of potential committees than your community association bylaws mention and your community currently has. If you are on the board of directors, use this list as the starting point for the beginning of a discussion about expanding the use of committees. If you are a homeowner, share the list with management and the board, and if you are so inclined, volunteer to serve as chair for one or more committees.

Better yet, whether you are on the board or an owner, consider chairing an ad-hoc committee whose mission it is to coordinate the formation of new committees. Such an ad-hoc committee would promote committee awareness, committee recruitment and committee education within the general membership of the community association in order to expand the scope and effectiveness of association committees. Embracing this tactic build a broader base of power necessary in order to move the community closer towards unity and community consciousness. Boards of directors that desire more unity and understand the advantages of creating a sense of community will welcome the help in pursuit of those goals. Boards that don't will oppose your efforts and, once again, that opposition should raise the red flag that your community association has been hijacked.

Here are some tips to help attract owners as you attempt to populate your community association committees:

- Have a 'Play Day' social event that showcases current committees and allows for brainstorming of future committees. Combine committee information with games (bingo, bunco, activities for children, etc.) and refreshments and food.
- Create a committee sign-up form and devote time at each board meeting to discuss the need for committee volunteers to those owners that attend the meeting.

- Post an online committee sign up form on the community website and have a separate section of the site devoted solely to committee work.
- Publish, on a regular basis, articles about association committees, committee updates and insert sign up forms in the association newsletters.
- Acknowledge the contributions of committee members and committee chairs on an on-going basis in the newsletter, on the website and at board meetings.
- At the Annual Meeting, take some time to publicly recognize committee members with a certificate of thanks, a gift certificate to a local business (that can be donated and those that donate receive mention in the newsletter and on the website, or some other token of the community's appreciation that can be taken home.
- Create a Volunteer of the Month, or a Volunteer of the Quarter, or even Volunteer of the Year award and publicize the winner in the newsletter, the website and at board meetings.
- Plant a tree in honor of the Volunteer of the Year award winner each year and publicize it.
- Send a press release to the local paper(s) announcing the winners of the Vounteer of the Month/Quarter/Year.
- Whenever an owner expresses confusion regarding an association issue, invite them to join the committee that would deal with that issue. If no committee exists, create one and invite the owner to join/chair it. Many negative association issues exist due to the distance between the perception of the owner and the reality of the true issue. Being part of a committee is also an education process that often brings owners closer to a true understanding of what is going on.

When considering what kinds of committees can be created—including those mentioned in the bylaws—here are some sample standing committees and a brief description of each. Keep in mind that this list is not intended as an all-emcompasing roster of committees every community association should have. But, should be considered according to the needs of the community.

- **Finance Committee**
- **Architectural Review Committee**
- **Rules & Regulations/Covenants Committee**
- **Landscape/Grounds Committee**
- **Parking Committee**
- **Security Committee**
- **Maintenance Committee**
- **Social Committee**
- **Communications Committee**
- **Newsletter Committee**
- **Website Committee**
- **Pool Committee**
- **Recreation Committee**
- **Clubhouse Committee**
- **Recycling Committee**
- **Welcoming/Hospitality Committee**
- **Neighborhood Watch Committee**
- **Environmental Committee**
- **Carpool Committee**
- **Travel Committee**
- **Clubs Committee**
- **Sunshine Committee**
- **Public Relations Committee**
- **Community Improvement Committee**
- **Civic Affairs Committee**
- **Community Garden Committee**
- **Recruitment Committee**

Finance Committee: The purpose of the **Finance Committee** is to oversee the financial activities of the community association. This includes development of the operating fund and reserve fund annual budgets, review and analysis of the monthly revenues and expenses of the organization, make recommendations to the board regarding the financial affairs of the organization and the impact of proposed activities, work with management to ensure that proper bids for the financial audit are obtained and made available to all homeowners and monitor the timely filing of all tax returns of the organization.

Architectural Control Committee: The purpose of the **Architectural Control Committee** is to review of all architectural submittals received by the community association. In addition, the Committee determines when a submittal is approved, denied or may make a request for re-submittal. The Committee may also inspect the community to assure homeowners are in compliance with the CC&R's and Design Guidelines.

Rules & Regulations/Covenants Committee: The Rules & Regulations/Covenant Committee serves as the rule enforcement branch of the community association board. Some of the jobs that the rules/covenant committee take on include finding outside counsel for preliminary work on issues like nonpayment of assessments or violation of association rules. The covenant committee acts as the judiciary entity for cases involving violations or infractions of rules and makes recommendations to the board; it can also be empowered to issue fines.

Landscape/Grounds Committee: The purpose of the Landscape/ Grounds Committee is to help assure the aesthetic integrity of the community by advising the Board of Directors regarding common area landscaping and compliance with association landscape maintenance guidelines. They may accompany the landscape contractor and management on regular inspections of community association common areas in order to determine items that need attention.

Parking Committee: The purpose of the Parking Committee is to enforce community parking regulations, guest parking guidelines and the towing policy of the community association. It can also be empowered to issue non-compliance fines.

Security Committee: The purpose of the **Security Committee** is to assist the Board of Directors by reviewing security and safety issues to ensure the community association continues to be a safe and secure place to live. Neighborhood watch responsibilities can also be assigned to the Security Committee. Access control coordination into and out of the community are also potential responsibilities.

Maintenance Committee: The purpose of the Maintenance Committee is to oversee maintenance and repair of improvements to the common areas and can include landscaping, the pool, parking lots, play areas, fences, entrance monuments, and lighting (including street lights), all in a manner consistent with the Declaration of Covenants, Conditions and Restrictions (CC&Rs).

Social Committee: The Social Committee is a group of residents that organize social events, outings, groups, and parties. The idea behind the Social Committee is to establish and build good relationships with residents and neighbors; to foster a cohesive community by organizing fun, interesting events for the entire community so neighbors can meet and socialize with each other. This is an extremely important committee because social events are one of the most effective ways to build resident attachment to their community—more on that later.

Communications Committee: The mission of the Communications Committee is to implement and oversee effective communications through a variety of media delivery systems with particular focus on dissemination of information from the Board of Directors as well as all other committees. The objective of this committee is for residents to receive and/or access information which enhances their knowledge and experience on issues relevant to the community. Newsletter and website responsibilities can be given to this committee if each do not have their own.

Newsletter Committee/Website Committee: The purpose of the Newsletter and Website Committee is to provide a means of communication with the members of the community association about the activities of the community, the Board, and the other individual members.

Pool Committee: The Pool Committee reviews and makes recommendations regarding pool operations, pool equipment and upkeep (maintenance and repair), pool conditions, contracts for services, contracts for repairs, and other pool related issues.

Recreation Committee: The purpose of the Recreation Committee is to develop and implement strategies for improving, expanding and upgrading community association recreational facilities and amenities.

Clubhouse Committee: The Clubhouse Committee is responsible for coordinating and scheduling all clubhouse functions, enforcing clubhouse regulations and implementing a reservation policy for owners to utilize the clubhouse for private functions.

Recycling Committee: The purpose of the Recycling Committee is to plan and implement community recycling programs.

Welcoming/Hospitality Committee: The primary goal and mission of the Welcoming/Hospitality Committee is to disseminate information that will help new onwers/residents transition into their new home and surroundings. This can include scheduling a personal visit, providing access information to the community website, letting them know about the newsletter (and allowing them the opportunity to be listed in it as a new resident), providing them with a current homeowner directory, encouraging participation in future community association functions and, above all else, answer any questions a new resident might have.

Neighborhood Watch Committee: The goal of the Neighborhood Watch is to increase and maintain the safety of the community by connecting neighbors to each other and looking out for strangers and suspicious activity. The Neighborhood Watch Committee is responsible for assigning block captain responsibilities and providing neighborhood crime fighting resources to community residents in conjunction with local law enforcement agencies.

Environmental Committee: For some community associations, the Environmental Committee takes on the responsibilities of both the Architectural Review Committee and the Landscape/Grounds Committee (defined above).

Carpool Committee: The Carpool Community coordinates and arranges for community residents to share rides from the community into surrounding business areas in order to get to and from work each day or to social events held outside the community.
Travel Committee: The purpose of the Travel Committee is to inform, educate, and create interest in travel by community association residents and to organize trips to destinations as requested by residents.
Clubs Committee: The Clubs Committee coordinates arrangement of community association facilities/amenities by the various clubs

within the community (i.e., poker club, bunco club, lawn bowling club, aerobics club, yoga club, reading club, red hat society, etc.).

Sunshine Committee: The Sunshine Committee coordinates efforts to help those within the community who are going through a transition from their 'normal' schedule. This may be a result of a new baby, family death, an extended illness, hospitalization, etc. Some of the help provided by the Sunshine Committee includes providing meals, transportation, wellness checks and other neighborly acts that benefit those in need. The Sunshine Committee can also coordinate community efforts for raising funds, collecting items or providing resources to charitable causes outside of the community.

Public Relations Committee: The Public Relations Committee can be the entity that publishes a newsletter when required and as appropriate and notifies the residents of public meetings held outside the community of interest to the community association. They can also be charged with creating and submitting press releases to local news outlets announcing community member achievements, announcements and/or information of interest.

Community Improvement Committee: The goal of the Community Improvement Committee is to promote community improvement and environmental protection and to organize projects concerning matters within the community association which are not within the duties of another committee.

Civic Affairs Committee: The duty of the Civic Affairs Committee is to be the community association's contact concerning matters of zoning, sheriff's department, fire department, rescue squad, and other civic departments. They can also maintain liaison with other community associations in the area.

Community Garden Committee: Shared gardens are an excellent way to encourage involvement and participation and grow vegetables that can either be enjoyed by residents and/or donated to local food banks. The Community Garden Committee would identify useable space within the community, recruit residents to help volunteer to create it and establish rules by which the community garden is operated under. Individual plots could be assigned to residents, or all those involved in the community garden could share responsibilities for the garden. Some experts even suggest that real estate values rise in community associations with shared gardens.

Recruitment Committee: The Recruitment Committee works in conjunction with all the established community association standing and ad-hoc committees in order to help populate them with volunteers. Some of the techniques used are to work with the Welcoming Committee, go door-to-door asking for volunteers, distributing committee information flyers and sign-up forms and coordinating committee sign-up social events with the Social Committee. Representatives of this committee can also attend board meetings in order to encourage owners in attendance to volunteer to serve on a committee.

There are also situations in which an ad hoc committee may be beneficial. Ad hoc committees are formed for a specific purpose which includes assisting with work and input on the budget, rules and regulations review, etc. The needs of the services of these types of committees terminates once their purpose/duties have been accomplished. Examples and brief descriptions of some of these ad-hoc committees are:

- Annual Meeting Committee
- Nominating Committee
- Rules Review Committee
- Audit Committee
- Re-Roofing Committee
- Street Slurry Committee
- Painting Committee

- Management Committee
- Contracts Committee
- Tree Trimming Committee
- Special Events Committee
- Annual Color Committee
- Clean-Up Day Committee

Annual Meeting Committee: Assists in the coordination and planning of the annual meeting and board of director election.

Nominating Committee: Solicits, identifies and recommends to the board qualified candidates to be placed on the ballot of the board of director election

Audit Committee: Solicits, interviews CPA firms/auditors and obtains bids for the annual financial audit and submits them to the board along with their recommendations.

Re-Roofing Committee: Solicits, interviews roofing companies, qualifies them (bonded, licensed, insured) and obtains bids for re-roofing projects and submits their recommendations to the board of directors.

Street Slurry Committee: Solicits, interviews street maintenance companies, qualifies them and obtains bids for street slurry/maintenance projects and submits them, along with their recommendations, to the board.

Painting Committee: Solicits, interviews painting contractors, qualifies them and obtains bids for community painting projects and submits their recommendations to the board.

Management Committee: Solicits, interviews management companies, qualifies them and obtains bids for community association management and presents them to the board.

Contracts/Vendor Committee: Reviews all current service contracts and makes recommendations to the board regarding renewal or researching of new service vendors.

Tree Trimming Committee: Conducts property inspections, identifies trees for trimming and works with landscaper/arborist regarding tree trimming. If a company other than the current landscape maintenance company is to be used for tree trimming, then bids are solicited, companies are interviewed and qualified and recommendations made to the board of directors.

Special Events Committee: Coordinates specific special events that are not the responsibility of the Social Committee. If there is no Social Committee, the Special Events Committee is formed prior to each planned social event and works to ensure its success.

Annual Color Committee: Works with the Landscape Committee and Landscaper in order to make recommendations regarding the installation of seasonal flowers throughout the community.

Clean-Up Day Committee: Oranizes and promotes a special community-wide event whose goal is to clean up the community by picking up litter, removing/painting over graffiti, sprucing up the the community common areas as appropriate.

From Ugly Duckling To Swan
If we compare the growth of unity within the community and community consciousness with that of the tale of the ugly duckling, we will find many similarities. The Ugly Duckling is a fairy tale by Danish poet and

author Hans Christian Andersen. The story tells of a homely little bird born in a barnyard who suffers abuse from his neighbors until, much to his delight (and to the surprise of others), he matures into a graceful swan, the most beautiful bird of all. The story of a community association that matures from a collection of isolated, self-serving owners into a community of owners—united in committee work—striving to create something larger than themselves that will improve the quality of their lives is indeed the story of moving from something ugly to something beautiful. In the beginning, no matter how much effort is expended in getting others to buy into the concept of community consciousness, the going will be slow and nearly imperceptible. However, in time, changes occur and, before you know it, the disinterested collection of owners becomes a beautiful, engaged community with active and effective committees. Embracing the work and the contributions of committees is to let go of the clinging obsession that some boards have regarding the belief that only 'they' know what is best for everyone. For community building to work, it must have the participation and utilize the contributions of many people, not the manipulations of just a couple self-serving board members. Self-serving behavior is ugly in creating community and establishing unity is beautiful.

The Bohemian-Austrian poet Rainer Maria Rilke's poem, The Swan, exemplifies the reality of anything that appears different than it truly is, and then, when we let go of the clinging that prevents it from growing, it moves closer to its natural state and it becomes exactly what it should be. In the beginning of creating community, we often see a clumsy, lumbering collection of individuals, each restrictive movement going nowhere, with little or no regard as to the consequences of their indifference upon those they share their community with (*This clumsy living that moves lumbering as if in ropes through what is not done*). As community consciousness expands and begins to include one owner and then another owner and so on, and we grow as a collection of caring neighbors and let go of the clinging of our old way of relating to each other (*And to die, which is the letting go of the ground we stand on and cling to every day*), we begin to see the graceful movement towards becoming a collection of individuals who are united in the beneficial understanding of their shared interests and the wisdom of pursuing common goals and objectives in order to improve the quality of their lives *(to be carried, each moment more fully grown, more like a king, further and further on)*.

The Swan *(Translation by Robert Bly)*

This clumsy living that moves lumbering
as if in ropes through what is not done,
reminds us of the awkward way the swan walks.
And to die, which is the letting go
of the ground we stand on and cling to every day,
is like the swan, when he nervously lets himself down
into the water, which receives him gaily
and which flows joyfully under
and after him, wave after wave,
while the swan, unmoving and marvelously calm,
is pleased to be carried, each moment more fully grown,
more like a king, further and further on.

COMPASSIONATE INVOLVEMENT

The Heart of Empowerment

"Anger makes you and other persons unhappy, and creates enemies and animosity. When you get angry it is very difficult to think in terms of compassion, for compassion is the opposite of anger."

Denma Locho Rinpoche

There is a story of a samurai, a Japanese warrior, who had the duty to avenge the murder of his overlord. When he cornered the man who had murdered his Overloard and he was about to strike him down with his samurai sword, the man, in the passion of terror, spat in the warrior's face. The samurai sheathed his sword and walked away. Why? Because the samurai was made angry and if he killed the man in anger, then it would have been a personal act. He had come to do another kind of act, an impersonal act of vengeance.

Reacting vs Responding

Creating community needs to be an impersonal act and those that create community need to act like the samurai and not *react* with anger when someone does something to upset you. When we perceive a threat it is a normal reaction to feel anger, but we can learn to take a step back and skillfully *respond* to a threatening person or situation. When we make it personal, we suffer defeats and setbacks just as if someone had done something to us individually and to *react* individually when a collective *response* is required is counter-productive to establishing community consciousness. As the Vietnamese Buddhist monk, Thich Nhat Hanh, reminds us in his book, Anger: Wisdom for Cooling the Flames: "When someone says or does something that makes us angry, we suffer. We tend to say or do something back to make the other suffer, with the hope that we will suffer less. We think, "I want to punish you, I want to make you suffer because you have made me suffer. And when I see you suffer a lot, I will feel better."

Frustration can quickly turn into anger and any choices fueled by anger are ultimately harmful choices and will not promote unity among the residents. Anger takes any situation out of the impersonal arena that community building requires and tends to make that situation personal. It does this by being motivated by a perception that a wrong has been committed against one's person. Personal anger seldom creates community-affirming solutions. Creating community should be an act of compassion, not anger.

Anger creates adrenaline in the body and it takes about 20 minutes for that adrenaline to leave the body. When we realize we are having an attack of adrenaline (heart racing, fists clenching, raging thoughts) we need to recognize that this is the moment to take a time-out and regain emotional control. I emphasize this technique because without instructions most people can't "think" when they are mad.

Metaphorically speaking, the "heart" of empowerment represents the attitude that should be embraced when choosing to act upon the realization that changes need to be made in the leadership of the community in order to move forward in accomplishing community consciousness. Any changes, large or small, will require heart. For our purposes, heart translates into a commitment to work towards solutions that are community-affirming and not community-destroying. It is easy to understand the frustration that is felt by owners when they come to realize that something is amiss and even easier to understand the desire to blame someone for whatever is wrong.

Assuming control of any community association should not be attempted with the intent to punish or demean those who may be responsible for the association's dysfunction. It should be attempted out of a deep understanding that creating community is best accomplished with the participation and support of all community members, even misguided board members. If we treat them with respect in our community building process it will send a message to everyone in the community that it is not the person(s) to blame for the dysfunction, it is the choices they made or the resident's own disinterest that helped create the dysfunction. In the end, everyone is still your neighbor—including the Lou Sifers of your community—and everyone has something to contribute, regardless of their history.

As Joseph Campbell, the mythologist, writer and lecturer told Bill Moyer on the PBS series, The Power of Myth, "Our life evokes our character and we find out more about ourselves as we go on. It is very nice to put ourselves in situations that will evoke our higher nature than our lower." Our higher nature is always best served when we put ourselves in a situation that affirms the positive values of community and inclusion. The question that everyone who wants to create community should ask themselves is, "What kind of neighbors will we be?" Will we be angry neighbors who point fingers and cast blame? Or, will we be responsible neighbors and make choices out of a desire to focus on issues that will unite everyone? We can take the response we see modeled by many politicians when they want to promote change: blame someone for the problem BEFORE suggesting a solution. Or we can refuse to accept that response and rise above it. We need to evoke our higher nature in order to model how positive change can be accomplished without blaming and set an example that others can follow. This is why we need to step back, not forward, when our blood boils and we want to react. We need to let ourselves cool down and respond wisely. Uniting with others, in any situation, demands that everyone involved have access to and are able to choose that part of themselves—their highest nature—when contributing their time and energy. The effort required to create community deserves nothing less.

Blaming others in order to rile up the masses and get them to storm the castle with you is all well and good—in theory or in the movies. The blame game may work to get the ball rolling by creating a target to go after (the party perceived as responsible for the community's dysfunction) but it will also create deep divisions within the community as owners either take sides or, due to the perceived unimportance of the matter, the owners decide to take a nap instead and adopt the 'wait and see' approach. Keep in mind that most of the owners are probably unaware that anything is wrong in the first place because, for the most part, they are not paying attention anyway. The latter option is probably the most popular for many owners. So, if we are going to have any success at all in creating community we have to wake up those napping owners without blaming anyone for interrupting their sleep.

The positive approach would be to focus the owner's attention on the prize, the goal, the direction we want to head towards, not on who is responsible for the unhealthy situation the community is currently in. Leadership may have chosen to evoke their lowest nature when they hijacked the association, whether conscious or not. Reacting to the challenge of trying to overcome the consequences of lower nature choices by making more choices which reflect our lower nature (such as blaming) is like fighting fire with fire—and the most successful form of fighting fire is by using water, its exact opposite. The most successful form of transforming anger is by using a cool head, which leads to understanding/compassion.

Focus Forward

There is a story that Tara Brach, Ph.D shares in her book "Radical Acceptance" that exemplifies the perils of feeling cut off from others in a community:

In one of the legends of the Holy Grail, Parsifal, a young knight on a quest, wanders into a parched and devastated land where nothing grows. When he arrives at the capital of this wasteland, he finds the townspeople behaving as if everything were normal. They are not wondering, "What horror has befallen us?" or, "What can we do?" Rather, they are dull and mechanical, as if under a spell.

Parsifal is invited into the castle where, to his surprise, he discovers the king lying in bed, pale and dying. Like the land around him, the monarch's life is waning. Parsifal is full of questions, but because he had been told by an older knight that asking questions was improper for one of his stature, he keeps quiet. The next morning he leaves the castle to continue on his journey, but he hasn't gone far before he meets the sorceress Kundri on the road. When she hears that Parsifal hadn't asked the king any questions, asked the king how he was feeling, she goes into a rage! How could Parsifal be so callous? He could have saved the king, the kingdom and himself by doing so.

Taking her words to heart, Parsifal returns to the wasteland and goes straight to the castle. Without even breaking his stride, he walks right up to where the king is lying on his couch. He kneels there and gently asks, "Oh, my lord, what aileth thee?" At that moment, the color comes back into the king's cheeks and he stands up, fully healed. Throughout the kingdom, everything comes to life. The people, newly awakened, talk with animation, laugh and sing together and move with a vigorous step. The crops begin to grow and the grass on the hills glows with the new green of spring.

When anyone feels cut off from others, as the king in this story was, their lives too can feel like a wasteland, empty of meaning, hollow and thin. And, that sense of alienation will eventually spread in a community and take the form of continued apathy and disinterest, the very things we are trying to correct. To blame anyone for anything is to cut them off from those doing the blaming. The heart of empowerment and the key to successfully freeing the community from dysfunctional leadership is rooted in healing not blaming, in inclusion not exclusion.

Blaming others is a waste of time and energy and models a habit of blaming when things don't go as they should that others will repeat when things don't go right for them (and things won't go as they should more often than not. It is the nature of the beast when trying to unite others). It's really all about the most effective use of the group's dynamic energy and where it needs to be directed in order to create community: focused ahead, not behind.

Overcoming the propensity to blame someone else when something goes wrong is inbred in the Western Judeo-Christian traditions that many of us were taught as we were growing up. Biblically, the very first thing to go wrong in the world (Adam and Eve disobeying God and eating of the tree of knowledge of good and evil) was dealt with through passing the buck and blaming. In Genesis, Chapter 3; Verses 9 through 13 it states:

"And the LORD God called unto Adam, and said unto him, Where [art] thou? And he said, I heard thy voice in the garden, and I was afraid, because I [was] naked; and I hid myself. And he said, Who told thee that thou [wast] naked? Hast thou eaten of the tree, whereof I commanded thee that thou shouldest not eat? And the man said, The woman whom thou gavest [to be] with me, she gave me of the tree, and I did eat. And the LORD God said unto the woman, What [is] this [that] thou hast done? And the woman said, The serpent beguiled me, and I did eat."

For the Adam, Eve, and the serpent, the blaming didn't go well as God punished them all. I venture to suggest that the consequences of blaming are the same now as they were in the beginning. *Blaming is an attitude that creates consequences, not rewards.* Metaphorically speaking, one has to wonder what would have happened to our world culture if, in the book of Genesis, Adam had manned up and taken responsibility for eating of the tree of knowledge of good and evil and let Eve and the serpent off the hook. Women (and snakes) have been paying for man's weaknesses and fears ever since. But, that's the subject of another book. Right now, what I want to emphasize is the absurdity of blaming, in community associations . . . and in life.

We cannot afford any energy being expended on making anyone in the community feel as if they are cut off from the rest of the community. This should apply not only to the owners who may be responsible for the need to create community consciousness, but also to any owners who may initially oppose community building efforts or are even just be disinterested. There is incredible power available when everyone feels connected and there is incredible power lost when any position that denies inclusiveness is embraced (blaming). Ostracizing anyone in the community, especially for acting in their own selfish interests, is in itself a selfish act on behalf of the community. The sitting board who may have hijacked the community association may not be the only ones who acted selfishly in the past or will act selfishly in the future as a new road to community is traveled. Don't let the community become what it is trying to break away from. Selfishness is extremely contagious in a group dynamic and can easily sabotage any efforts to unify community members because its effects are contrary to our goals. When we choose to cut off anyone from our sense of community, in effect, we cut off everyone.

There are many components to a hijacked or dysfunctional community and each of which has its own history and causes and everyone in the community is affected by them. Separating others by blaming them for everything will not heal the community, being thankful that healing has begun and having compassion towards everyone in the community will.

ESCAPING THE HIJACKERS

The Loss of Empowerment

". . . in the absence of genuine leadership, (people) listen to anyone who steps up to the microphone. They want leadership. They're so thirsty for it they'll crawl through the desert toward a mirage, and when they discover there's no water, they'll drink the sand."
Lewis Rothschild in The American President

The response that the President had for Lewis in The American President was, "People don't drink the sand because they're thirsty. They drink the sand because they don't know the difference." The next two chapters will both aim to help you recognize the differences between genuine leadership and dysfunctional leadership. Genuine leadership works towards the betterment of all, dysfunctional leadership does not. To do this we will focus on identifying when a community has dysfunctional leadership or has been hijacked. In the next chapter we will define the qualities of genuine leadership and how to increase leadership skills.

Before we examine some of the characteristics of a hijacked community more closely, I need to explain that "hijacked" is a word that has a lot of power. I chose to use the term "hijacked" in order to take advantage of that power and get your attention. *However, most community associations get hijacked very subtlety and without attention.* Often it happens unintentionally as the result of a powerful personality in a position of authority. Other times a hijacking occurs because the board takes on an enabling relationship with whoever is president or manager. Certainly there are instances of hijacking a community that are well-planned assaults, but for the most part, *hijackings are simply the result of owners failing to pay attention to what is going on regarding the management of their community association.* Functionally speaking, you can interchange the word 'dysfunctional' with 'hijacked' at any time and the meaning still comes across. Regardless of the cause, it is a situation that has a solution, or series of solutions, and should not create any more animosity among owners than it already has.

One should not confuse a strong, focused and engaged board of directors with a board that has seized control for its own nefarious purposes. If there are opportunities for involvement, frequent solicitations for input and attempts being made to keep the owners informed, be thankful, not suspicious. Also, if the community association is professionally managed by a reputable and competent company, then the internal policies of the management company and how they conduct business should prevent any hijackings. Unfortunately, there are still misguided, manipulative boards and management companies who would rather hire inexperienced managers who see their job as serving at the board's whim rather than as being a valuable source of guidance and direction. Both instances are ripe for hijacking.

I realize that some of you are reading this book, not because of the flashy cover, but because want to improve the quality of community in your community association. Your association has not been hijacked nor is it mismanaged or dysfunctional. You may be the member, or president, of a very strong board of directors that truly works at doing their best to carry out their fiduciary responsibilities. This chapter will likely reinforce many of the leadership choices you have already made in order to be where you are at today.

Other readers, however, may not be happy with their current community association leadership and are searching for answers in order to help make a difficult situation better. You may be a member of the board with a manipulative president, or an owner who feels as if community association leadership is not listening to the owner's concerns, or the president of the community association that can never seem to get the board to agree on anything. Is the current challenging situation due to a hijacking? Maybe it is. Maybe it isn't. It is important to keep in mind that the hijacking of a community association is not a black or white condition. There are levels and depths of hijacking, each of which have different responses that are appropriate in order to correct the situation. This chapter will shed some light on just what your particular malady may be and help you realize the appropriate remedy in order to heal it.

Some dysfunctional community association dynamics can simply be attributed to ineffective leadership, poor professional management, and/or ignorance of community dynamics. However, one of the most frustrating community association situations is when leadership is seized and manipulated in order to further the betterment of a minority of homeowners while the burdens of those advantages are felt by the vast majority of community residents—as in the story of the Shady Dealings HOA. The community association is hijacked. The hijackers can be individual board members (usually the one who values force over power), a majority of the board, an entire board of directors, even a community association manager or management company. Whatever the reason, before we learn how to correct the situation, let's take a closer look at just what is really going on when a community association is hijacked or identify whether or not it is just the victim of ineffective leadership.

Due to the nature of community association hijackings, there is never just one event that causes it. In fact, due to the disinterested and apathetic attitude of many owners, a hijacking can occur without anyone even noticing. One of the analogies that I have used (and borrowed from my mentor, Jan Lhotka) is that management of community associations is akin to the function of the electric company. As long as the lights come on, no one even notices that the electric company even exists or what they do unbeknownst to their customers behind the scenes in order to ensure that the lights keep coming on every time you flip the light switch to "on". Leadership of a community association can work in much the same way. As long as the grass is cut in the common area, the weeds are removed, the pool is heated and the roofs don't leak, many owners are content to just let the board and/or management company continue on their merry way—regardless of what is happening behind closed doors and the decisions they are unaware of. But, god forbid there comes the day when you flip the switch on and . . . no lights! Hell hath known no fury greater than the fury of a person deprived of their television, microwaveable dinner, computer or hair dryer.

Community association leadership is really no different. Everything is hunky-dory until the special assessment bill is delivered in the mail, the non-compliance notice arrives demanding you remove the bamboo screen from your balcony, weeds take over the common area landscaping or the spa quits working. It is then that people sit up and take notice . . . at least until the spa is fixed, the special assessment is paid or the weeds are removed. Then, it's back to La-La Land and Hunky-Doryville.

There are some homeowners who, once they take notice, start to look into just why there is a special assessment and the status of the association reserve funds, or they read the architectural guidelines in order to find out if bamboo screens are forbidden, or begin to ask questions as to why the association's pool equipment requires so much maintenance, or the common areas are so routinely neglected. Those inquiries often lead to findings that point out the fact that things could be run much better than they currently are and the newly-enlightened owner decides to get more involved. At some point in the history of most every community association ever created, *dissatisfaction with leadership has inspired greater participation, if only by one single homeowner. The key is to be able to refocus that dissatisfaction into positive choices that benefit everyone in the community and not just them.*

We don't have to go any further than the story of Lou Sifer to provide an example of someone who chose to vent his frustration at a perceived wrong by stirring up the pot of disinterest within the community and spicing it up with his own brand of justice: Gathering support from other owners, being elected to the board of directors, imposing his will upon the rest of the board and pushing through changes in the management company and security service. It is highly unlikely that his pattern of leadership will change once his initial goals are accomplished and, given the grass roots effort he undertook to obtain control of the board of directors, he will most likely continue to force his self-serving agenda upon the community. It is possible that other owners will take notice, rise up and repeat Lou's personal empowerment efforts and dispatch Lou from the board in the same manner that he dispatched the former board. This cycle of obtaining and manipulating community association leadership can continue indefinitely. In the meantime, community building efforts are impossible because the owners of the community keep getting divided in their loyalties and move further and further apart in their sense of unity. This type of community association leadership dynamic is an example of serial hijacking and is repeated over and over and over again.

As I have already warned, embracing that strategy to create community consciousness (getting enough people pissed off so that they unite in order to fight injustice and in the process create a sense of unity, if only temporarily) is time consuming and unwise in the long run because it reinforces negative problem-solving habits. However, there is always a chance that a large enough group of owners get so fed up with this vicious cycle of leadership that they unite under the banner of 'community' and begin to make effective long-term changes for the sake of the entire association.

So, how does anyone know when their community association has been hijacked? Other than the examples that I have already listed, here are some general signs that it may be time to plan a takeover. This list is not by any means all-inclusive and there are some well run community associations that may even exhibit some of these traits. The point here is to present a dysfunctional leadership style that reflects the most common characteristics of a hijacked community association:

- Board members and their positions on the board have not changed in years
- A lack of transparency in board of director decisions, actions and financial disclosures
- Inconsistencies in board election procedures/results
- No substantial communication from the association other than legally mandated notices
- Input from owners is discouraged or ignored
- Lack of accessibility to community association leadership
- Inequality in access to community association information from the management company
- Board members/management pushing services affiliated with them upon the community association without soliciting/ reviewing competitive bids or services
- Management representatives making decisions that should be made by the board of directors
- Lack of leadership honesty

Some states have addressed many of these issues by passing legislation requiring more transparency, requiring homeowners be allowed at board meetings and permitting reasonable access to corporate records.

However, at present there is no such thing as a community association police department to call in order to have violators arrested. Any complaints have to be handled through timely and expensive legal channels and will usually end up creating more division among owners, which is the opposite of our goal to create community. So, the most likely and least expensive burden of making effective changes ultimately falls upon the owners of the community association themselves.

The main reason that community associations get hijacked in the first place is because there is usually no one within the community who is paying attention to what is going on, other than the board. Even among the board there may be members that are disengaged from making decisions due to repeated absences from meetings or, as I said, enabling other board members to make decisions for them. There is no Parsifal to ask "What aileth thee?" The grass gets mowed, the pool gets cleaned, assessment checks get cashed, the association seems to be running smoothly. In fact, the neighbor's dog barking while you are trying to nap probably generates more frustration than the fact that the board has been spending money intended for the street repair reserve fund on planting rose bushes outside every home in the community, or whatever the current pet project is of Mrs. or Mr. Board President. Hyperbole? A little, but I think you get the point. Community Associations cannot get hijacked in the first place without the tacit approval of the community members. *Get owners to start paying attention and good things happen . . . eventually.*

The Talking Cure

Let's look more closely at some of the symptoms of a community that has been hijacked. Some associations may experience only one of the symptoms and other associations may experience more or all of them. Regardless, if any of the following symptoms are experienced, there is something happening that shouldn't be. Although I will list some suggested solutions for each symptom, many of the solutions have already been addressed in the chapters on communication tools, committees and the faces of empowerment. Sometimes, the solution will require nothing more than informing the board of directors or management that it is a concern. If you don't ask, you don't receive. *So, for all of these symptoms, consider the first option of addressing it to be simply the act of talking to the board/management about it.* Depending upon the maturity of the parties involved, they will acknowledge the concern and implement remedies, or they will deny anything is wrong and become even more fixated on isolating owners from the decision-making process. If the latter choice is made, more serious efforts will need to be made by the owners to change the situation and begin creating community. Either way, use this opportunity to begin your involvement in your community association.

Here are some brief descriptions of the previously mentioned symptoms of hijacked associations and a few possible healing solutions:

Board members and their positions on the board have not changed in years: This is either the most telling sign that the association has been hijacked, or an example of a community association in which no one cares enough about to volunteer to serve on the board of directors. Either way, it keeps a leadership style in place which is most likely flawed, otherwise there would be more interest in and attention paid to the community association and the board of directors. It is the exception and not the rule that the board is so effective and popular with the owners that they are voted back into office again and again and again. Usually either no one is interested in serving on the board each and every year or the board controls the election process and doesn't want to leave. Many of these types of hijacked associations have very few committees and the ones they do have are populated by the board members.

Solution: Get more owners involved and help the board recruit new owners to serve on existing committees. Suggest that new committees be established that focus on issues that existing committees do not cover. Start with a handful of owners who are willing to go door-to-door and solicit committee members.

When the time for the Annual Meeting arrives, ensure that there are other candidates than existing board members running for open board positions. If the committee recruitment efforts were successful, there should be numerous potential board candidates identified and willing to serve. If the existing board refutes all efforts at expanding committees or handing over control over potential board candidates, consider soliciting Proxies and having owners sign over their voting privileges to the new board candidate(s) and NOT the existing board. Other solutions involve getting more owners to attend board meetings and voice their concerns about the lack of leadership change in the community. The board's response to those concerns will be an honest indicator as to whether they have indeed hijacked the association or just didn't realize others wanted to get involved.

When To Get Legal Help

If the board continues to deny the right of owners to run for the board or manipulates proxies/ballots then research the governing documents (Bylaws) and determine the extent of their authority. If presented with evidence that they are operating outside of the scope of the governing documents, and they continue to refuse to budge, consult with an attorney that specializes in community association law and consider taking legal remedies. Otherwise, although it does give the community a public relations black eye, consider taking the story to the public and contact local newspapers and television stations and share your story in order to apply public pressure to the board.

Finally, when the annual meeting arrives, consider establishing an informal committee whose sole purpose is to ensure that owners submit their signed proxy and ballot. In these kinds of situations, the more owners that participate in the election process without turning over their votes to the board, the greater the chance that other candidates can be elected.

A lack of transparency in board of director decisions, actions and financial disclosures: If the board of directors, or management company, does not provide access to approved board meeting minutes, will not provide audit, association balance sheet and/or profit/loss information when requested and/or never allows owners to speak at board meetings, you just might have been hijacked. Most states require certain disclosures on a yearly basis that the boards must comply with. If these disclosures are not sent, it may be the fault of the management company if they are managed by one, or it may be because the board does not want others to know what is going on. Either way, it is wrong.

Solution: Make formal written requests of the board and/or management company for copies of the approved minutes that are available and any audit summaries as required by law, if applicable. If the association is professionally managed, meet with management company executives in order to explain what is happening. If the community association is self-managed, meet with the manager and ask for an explanation. If there is none, and there is no plan to provide information to the owners in the future, attempt to recruit more owners to press for disclosure in order to increase pressure on the board/management. Considering there is most likely legislation requiring disclosure, legal remedies should be considered if nothing else works.

Inconsistencies in board election procedures/results: There are a number of issues that can signify inconsistencies in election/voting procedures/results.

- The board often reports that quorum has been obtained and that they possess a majority of votes signed over by owners even though they refuse to provide proof.
- Those responsible for tallying votes and qualifying ballots are related to board members.
- Proxies and/or ballots are routinely dismissed and not counted for reasons that are not included in governing documents or addressed by legislation (i.e., owner's dog barks at night, owner has a history of being in non-compliance for failing to put trash cans out of sight after pickup, owner is even one day late in paying monthly assessment).
- The board continually claims that quorum is never obtained at annual meetings and subsequent adjourned annual meetings (even though the quorum requirement is reduced significantly after failing to obtain quorum at the initial annual meeting per the governing documents) and cancels the board of directors election and leaves the existing board in place for another term.
- There is no significant effort made by the board/management to recruit owners to run for election to the board so that when vacancies come up and there are no candidates to vote on at the annual meeting, the board is allowed to appoint board members and appoints their friends.

Solution: Solicit other owners not affiliated with the board to volunteer to serve as voting inspectors in order to ensure that quorum is obtained and the voting process is legitimate. There are also outside services available for hire that conduct HOA voting according to governing documents. If the board is opposed to accepting any owner volunteers to help conduct the election than that is surely a red flag. Management companies also routinely provide extra personnel to assist with elections if requested.

Potential board candidates need to be sure and let the board and management know of their interest and intent to run for an open board position as soon as possible in order to ensure that they name appears on the ballot. It is also important that potential candidates understand the importance of introducing themselves to the owners of the community association and establish a platform that they can ask the owners to support by voting for them. Naturally, a "Meet the Candidates" night would be the perfect forum for such an introduction, but if the board is set on maintaining control of who is on the board, they probably won't approve an official event. Other options would be to go door-to-door, or organize your own meeting at a private home (similar to an open house) that owners can visit during the day or evening in order to meet the candidate.

If, despite submitting their name and completing any required candidate questionnaire, their name does not appear on the ballot, owners need to know that they have the right to write-in the candidates name and vote for them that way. If the board controls the process of selecting board candidates to run for open seats, write-in voting may be the only way to counter their efforts to manipulate the voting process (as long as the board is also not the only entity responsible for counting votes, and if that is the case, you can only hope they are honest in their vote tallying).

The key to ensuring a legitimate, accurate and fair election is to make sure that the persons responsible for determining whether quorum is established and ballot are counted are not associated with the board or any prospective board candidates. The most powerful of all measures to ensure that voting is done correctly is to have all the owners participate in the voting process AND attend the annual meeting. It is highly unlikely any shenanigans can be implemented with so many witnesses present.

No substantial communication from the association other than legally mandated notices: If, the owners are not given the opportunity to receive information about the activities, decisions, and issues that face their community association then there can be no board of director accountability. The board of directors can do anything they want because they have made sure that no one is watching them.

Solution: Find out when and where board meetings are being held and attend them. Recruit other owners to attend them with you so that the board understands that others are interested in what they are doing. Volunteer to serve on a communications committee and suggest effective tools to keep owners informed. If the board does not have or is willing to release any funds to support communication efforts, consider establishing a communication tree within the community: A group of owners willing to go door-to-door and inform owners of pending events, issues and board decisions. Usually there is some location in the community for a bulletin board (pool area, clubhouse, parking area). Ask the board to agree to post a bulletin board so that information can be posted in order to provide information to owners on a regular basis. If there are assessment billing statements being sent out to owners by management, ask if information can be included in with each statement.

If the board refutes any efforts to increase communication to owners, that should be another red flag being raised. Consider making a board member change at the next annual meeting and solicit volunteers to run for open board seats and establish a grass roots effort to ensure that owners participate in the annual meeting and board member election by going door-to-door.

Input from owners is discouraged or ignored: If the board is not interested in listening to owners, they are not interested in empowering them. It's time for new board members, period.

Solution: Begin recruiting potential board candidates from the ownership who understand the value of listening to owners, soliciting their help in identifying community problems and assist in solving them. If the board attempts to manipulate the voting procedure, see the information on that hijacking symptom already addressed.

Lack of accessibility to community association leadership: If the board and/or management seem to operate under the cloak of invisibility, one has to wonder just what they are up to. There can be no transparency if the community association leaders do not allow owners to attend board meetings (although many states require an open forum session) or management does not return phone calls or emails. Realistically, the only time the members of the board are official board members is during the board of directors meeting. At all other times, they are just neighbors. That is why there is management. Management should function as the hub of communication for the board of directors. All communications should go through management. If management is not forwarding communications to the board, it is a management problem and should be addressed by the board. If the board is receiving communications but not acknowledging or instructing management to answer them, then it is a board problem and should be addressed by the owners—possibly with the help of management.

Solution: If it is a board problem, begin the process of recruiting owners to run for open board seats at the next election and help create a campaign strategy that will increase the odds that more owners will participate in the annual meeting and voting process. If focused on the issues, those owners should support new blood on the board and vote accordingly.

Inequality in access to community association information from management company: If the management company takes sides and cooperates with one side of owners and ignores another, or refuses to provide public information to owners who are opposed to the current board, the management company may be hijacking the association in favor of the board or group of owners they believe will support the renewal of their management contract.

Solution: Contact the community manager's supervisor and share the problem with them. It could be the result of a manager with misguided allegiances or one who has gone rogue. It is hard to imagine any professional management company supporting denial of access to records that are legally available to the public. If the problem continues, confront the board of directors in order to determine if the manager is just following direction. It is possible that the board knows nothing about it and can correct the problem. If they don't, work on having sympathetic owners put on the ballot at the next annual meeting, implement an effective election campaign and make sure other management companies are asked for bids when the current management company's contract is up for renewal.

If the information being requested is considered to be public documents of record and you cannot get them from the management company, look into other sources (Secretary of State) and consult with an attorney that specializes in community association law in order to find out what can be done in order to obtain the required information.

Board members/management pushing services affiliated with them upon the community association without soliciting/reviewing competitive bids or services: Whenever a member of the board or the management company is affiliated with a service vendor and brings a motion before the board approving the use of that vendor/ service without also providing competing bids, it is certainly a form of hijacking the community association. Some large management companies have created service divisions, or affiliated companies (landscape maintenance, construction services, collection services, website maintenance, etc.) that they argue gives the board more control over the quality of the service provided to the community. However, when those affiliated services are pushed upon the board without the opportunity for the existing service provider to respond or compete—or other companies are not asked for competing bids—that is a form of hijacking and only serves to increase the profit center of the management company. Quality or supervision of service is really secondary otherwise there would not be a problem with competitive bids being solicited. When a board member asks the board to approve a new landscape company, for example (which just so happens to be the employer of his wife's brother) without soliciting or obtaining other bids, that too is a form of hijacking. The bottom line is that ALL service providers that are hired by the community association should be chosen through the process of obtaining competitive bids and vetting those companies in order to make the best business decision possible and reflect a desire to do what is right for the entire community, not what is right for a board member's family or the management company.

Solution: Ensure that there are at least three (3) competitive bids solicited for any service contracts awarded by the board of directors. If you are a homeowner, attend board meetings and look at the agenda which should be available (in some states it is a requirement that the agenda be available at least four (4) days prior to the meeting. If the board is going to be voting on the approval of a service contract at the meeting, use the open forum session to ensure that there is more than one bidder. If there isn't, ask the board why, and let them know that approving service contracts without competitive bids is not acceptable business conduct in any industry and they may be in violation of complying with the fiduciary responsibilities granted them by the governing documents and the state. Big words, but they may be enough for the board to table the contract approval and instruct management to obtain other bids for review.

Management representatives making decisions that should be made by the board of directors: If the community association manager or other management company representatives are making operating decisions that are beyond the scope of their contract and/or state law, you are being hijacked. Management may argue that the board is weak, ineffective and seldom attends board meetings in order to make those decisions, but that is not a valid reason to make maintenance or financial decisions that they have not been empowered to make.

Solution: Confront management company supervisors and the board of directors in order to determine exactly what is going on. The board may be weak and unavailable, if so, management still should not be making those decisions. Instead they should be working to get more engaged owners on the board that are able to attend meetings and make the kind of business decisions that only the board of directors can legally make. This kind of hijacking is extremely rare, but does happen, especially in small associations with few owners serving on the board.

Lack of leadership honesty: If the board of directors is telling the owners one thing and then doing something else, this is a hijacking. The only reasons the board would be willing to tell the owners lies is because the truth would expose some previous mistake or some future plan to take advantage of the owners knowledge (or lack thereof) and/or common assets. It could be as simple as promising not to trim trees and then having it done, to something as complicated as assuring owners that the reserves are being funded when in fact they are not.

Solution: Confront the board about the discrepancies in word and action and inform management. Take the previously discussed measures to get other owners elected to open board seats at the next annual meeting. If the discrepancy is severe, recruit owners who would be willing to serve on the board and attend board meetings and demand all or part of the board resign immediately and appoint new members to serve until the annual meeting and board of director election. It's worth a shot.

Final Thoughts on Escaping the Hijackers

Information is knowledge and knowledge is power. Regardless of the causes or reasons for a community association being hijacked, the ultimate solution is to inform the owners of the issues and allow them to obtain the knowledge that is necessary in order for there to be a shift in power: A shift that power to the majority of owners and removes it from a self-serving minority of owners.

Many of us who have lived in community associations that were led by dysfunctional leadership would like to believe that, like Nelle, we were tied up on the railroad tracks by Snidely Whiplash against our will and await the arrival of Dudley DoRight to save us. In reality, there are no victims and there is no Snidely Whiplash. Dysfunctional leadership can never happen in a community association that is united, engaged in the issues and active in community association affairs. When that doesn't happen, it is easy to get hijacked. Let's now focus on the more positive elements of creating community: The effective community association leader.

LEADERSHIP

The Intelligence of Empowerment

"This is the true joy of life, the being used up for a purpose
recognized by yourself as a mighty one; being a force of nature
instead of a feverish, selfish little clod of ailments and grievances,
complaining that the world will not devote itself to making you happy.
I am of the opinion that my life belongs to the community, and as long
as I live, it is my privilege to do for it whatever I can. I want to be
thoroughly used up when I die, for the harder I work, the more I live."

George Bernard Shaw

Coming to the choice of deciding to serve your community association and accept the role of a leader is really a reflection of an innate longing to contribute to something that you are a part of but is larger than just yourself. Many people choose to volunteer to serve others at hospitals, homeless shelters, hospices or any number of service-oriented organizations whose primary aim is to help others. The motivation to serve your community association should not be all that different. It is about helping improve the quality of your neighbor's lives even if your neighbors don't understand the powerful impact of positive community association management because they may be indifferent or ignorant of its contribution to their well-being. How other people think about the community association will certainly impact how successful any community association leadership position will be in the beginning of any community building efforts, but it definitely should not be considered when deciding whether or not your community is worthy enough for your time, energy or skills. It is!

We all have this inner calling to be a part of community. Bo Lozoff, the Director of the Human Kindness Foundation, put it in perspective when he said that a sense of community is part of our deepest nature. We are born into a family that lives within a tribe, a village, town, or city. (As I write this a devastating earthquake and tsunami hit Japan a little over two weeks ago and spawned a world-wide awareness of just how fragile our life is and how connected we all are.) When earthquakes or hurricanes or floods come, they affect our neighbors as well as us, and we are reminded of our need to help each other and to care for each other's well-being. As infants and children, we all develop natural selfishness to some degree, but it remains very important to us to feel a sense of community and a sense of our own place in it.

Service and community are inextricable. Service, in the largest sense, could be defined simply as the manifestation of our inborn concern for the common good. If we do not allow our desires and fears to get out of hand, we do naturally care about the welfare of others—others in our family, our community, our nation, our world. Because this is natural, it leads to happiness and meaningfulness. If we allow ourselves to be led astray by the competitive individualism of our day, so that all our attention is focused on our own wants and needs and goals, then we will not be happy no matter how much material success we achieve.

From this point of view, service and the pursuit of happiness are intimately linked. A classic Tibetan way of putting this is, "All suffering comes from cherishing ourselves more than others. All happiness comes from cherishing others more than ourselves." In other words, though we naturally have both selfish and altruistic leanings, we are advised to put the altruistic first if we know what's good for us. Jesus echoed this advice when he said, "Greater Love hath no man than this:

That he lay down his life for his fellow man." Note the words "Greater Love." It stands to reason that a person feeling such great love would tend toward the happy and meaningful side of life. Note also that laying down our lives need not be confined to taking a bullet for somebody but may be another way of agreeing with George Bernard Shaw that "my life belongs to the community."

As a leader, being aware of that relationship between service and happiness is vital because it is a relationship you share with everyone within your community. It is a point of unity. Even though you may not have been unaware of it, the choice to lead your community association is a reflection of your choice to unify and empower your community and thus bless yourself by blessing others.

The next step on our journey is to further define the traits of a genuine leader and how those traits translate into empowering the people around them. Creating community demands that as many people as possible are given the opportunity to participate and contribute in the community building process, a process that is ongoing and without end. Motivating those people to make a conscious choice to risk greater involvement in their community and with their neighbors is one of the biggest challenges of creating community. We've already visited some examples of ineffective leadership and the consequences that dysfunctional leadership has on a community association. We've also looked at some of the ways in which empowerment is best achieved. Now, let's examine how effective leadership works and discover some methods to increase our own leadership skills through the identification of various motivational factors.

Qualities of a Leader: Motivating Others

Becoming a leader is a learning process that involves understanding what motivates people. If everyone were motivated by the same thing, then becoming a leader would be so much easier because all a person would have to do in order to become a leader is offer that same "thing" to everyone. Gaining the approval of others is a general motivator because it is human nature. In fact, approval and disapproval by others become significant mitigators of our natural selfishness, and that is entirely appropriate, so long as approval does not become our sole motivational system. We are individuals, but we are also communal beings. These two roles are not at odds; rather they provide crucial checks and balances for each other.

However, there are also specific factors that are even more effective in motivating others. Everyone has unique personal "things" that motivate them. *The real challenge in becoming a genuine leader is learning how to distinguish what unique motivating factors will work in getting so many people with different values, beliefs, experiences and skills to unite in the pursuit of a common goal or goals.* The desire to serve is certainly one motivational factor that everyone shares, even if they don't realize it. An example of a general motivational factor might be one's desire to help protect our country. Most people share it, but not everyone acts upon it and joins the military. Now, if your father had a personal experience with the military and you were surrounded by that culture as you grew up, you also have a specific motivational factor that will, most likely, be the biggest contributor to helping you make a decision to enlist in the military.

Let's take that example and apply it to a community association. One of the best ways to begin creating community in an association is an effective neighborhood watch program. Neighborhood watch is one of the most effective devices to curb neighborhood crime and to unite owners because its basic principle is neighbors watching out for each other. Everyone has a general motivating factor regarding the desire to protect their home. However, that general motivating factor may not be enough to get owners involved in neighborhood watch. What we need is to employ a specific motivational factor that will increase the chances of owners participating in neighborhood watch. In this instance, it isn't that a member of their family had an experience with neighborhood watch that will inspire their participation (as in the example about the military), but it could be that other members of the community have had positive experiences with neighborhood watch and by sharing those experiences will motivate participation. Or, it could be that a neighbor shares their experiences with having their own home broken into that will trigger involvement. It might be the result of a presentation by law enforcement representatives about how and why neighborhood watch works that does the trick. The more motivational factors a leader identifies, the more effective their leadership will be.

As was mentioned before, the greatest obstacle we face in creating community is an overall attitude of passive disinterest that a majority of owners share when it comes to issues involving their community association. What stirs their passion and interest in their community is usually not a deep desire to contribute their time and energy to the betterment of their neighbor's lives, it is whenever something happens that they don't expect, usually something they perceive of as being negative. They receive a non-compliance notice, a special assessment statement, the neighbor's dog poops in their driveway, or the entry gate is stuck open. Unfortunately, the passion that is stirred in those instances is not the kind that is easily harnessed and used in order to further our community building efforts. However, it is a starting point.

Encouraging Meaningful Participation
An effective community association leader will recognize that if something happens within the dynamic of managing a community association that gets people to engage with the board or management, regardless of whether it is positive or negative, then there is an opportunity to expand that engagement into meaningful participation. There is an opportunity for a conversation. In looking at the underlying reasons for the owner's engagement through a wider lens, the effective

leader can identify the important motivating factors that they can use in order to expand the owner's participation in creating community.

For example, the owner who contacts management to complain about the neighbor's dog pooping on their driveway has shown an interest in getting greater compliance with community rules (general motivating factor), even if it is because he keeps stepping in poop when he goes out to get the paper each morning (specific motivating factor). The issue may be specific (dog poop on driveway) but at the heart of the issue is the fact that someone is not complying with one of the community's rules regarding pet owner responsibilities and proper pet waste clean-up. Realizing that by helping the owner solve his dog poop issue is best accomplished by enlisting the owner's participation in helping to solve non-compliance issues in general, leadership can take the opportunity to recruit the owner to volunteer to serve on a rules committee or pet committee.

Many owners may simply want management to deal with the problem so they can go back to their nap, so to speak. However, if the increased role of committee member were presented in a win-win scenario to the owner, employing all motivational factors at the leader's disposal, then it would increase the chances that, instead of just another pissed off owner complaining, the community can benefit from someone who understands the frustrations of non-compliance. Their participation may lead to greater awareness of non-compliance issues throughout the community and provide a sense of satisfaction to the owner that they are helping to make the community better, one pile of dog poop at a time. Once that sense of satisfaction is achieved, it reinforces continued participation, not just from that owner, but from everyone who sees the positive changes that can take place when someone chooses to get involved.

Positive participation is a model for others to witness that can lead to greater participation by other owners. The problem that many community associations have is that leadership does not do a very good job of helping people to want to help their community, so the relationship between positive participation equaling greater participation is never established. For the most part, a complaining owner simply remains a complaining owner.

Exercise: Think of all the complaints that can be reported by owners regarding community association issues. Solving the specific complaint addresses the specific motivating factor. Now, brainstorm ways in which each specific complaint can be addressed within the structure of the community association. In the example used above, the complaint is dog poop and the opportunity for owner involvement is by participating on the rules or pet committee.

The purpose of this exercise is not really to have a road map to follow regarding what happens whenever an owner complains, but to get you to start thinking differently about how to increase owner participation. If the owner felt strongly enough to complain about an issue, use those feelings to continue the conversation and, hopefully, owner participation will increase. It won't happen every time, but it will happen more times than when compared to doing nothing will.

How To Understand People Better

Learning to understand people better is one of the most important leadership skills you can have. Even the very basics will give you the ability to make sound decisions and develop incredible insight into people's lives. With practice, your ability to understand the core motivations, desires, and thoughts of others can become incredibly accurate and that understanding can be used in order to help lead others into community.

The first step is gaining a general understanding of the makeup of others and surprisingly . . . ourselves. Without understanding the walls people build up around themselves, as well as the barriers that we put in our own way, we will never be able to successfully read other people.

People are Like Onions: When it comes to revealing ourselves to others, people are very much like a four-layered onion. The outermost layer is that part of our personality that we reveal to strangers—the most superficial aspects of who we really are. An example of this can be seen when we talk with a neighbor we don't know but meet on the street walking our dog. Trivial topics like the weather, current events, sights and sounds around us are typical things we feel willing to talk about.

Around our friends and some acquaintances we feel comfortable enough to peel back that outermost layer to reveal the next one. For example, if you were chatting with a friend this time, you would probably feel more comfortable revealing more about yourself. Your attitudes towards the community, certain emotions and your general thoughts about life are some of the things that might come up in conversation.

The third layer is reserved for those with whom we have an intimate relationship with, such as a close friend or spouse. In many cases, intimate relationships take time to develop, and with that time, trust is earned. Imagine now walking your dog with your spouse or significant other. The depth of what you reveal this time is much greater than any previous layer. Your goals, personal problems, and fears and so on, all fall within this layer.

The fourth and innermost layer contains that part of ourselves that we don't share with anyone. It contains our deepest and sometimes darkest thoughts and secrets that we would rather not acknowledge. The fact that we are trying to come to terms with many of these things ourselves makes us not comfortable sharing them with others.

The extent to which you can 'read' or understand someone is determined by how many of their layers you're able to get them to reveal. *And here's a little secret: a person will reveal their layers in direct proportion to you revealing yours.* This is the onion theory in a nutshell.

Removing our own Barrier: The second part of preparing ourselves to understand people better involves removing the barrier that keeps us from accurate 'people-reading'. That barrier is our prejudices.

When people think of prejudice, mostly the racial kind comes to mind. Although a part of it, this is not entirely what I'm talking about here. Anytime you make an opinion, whether it is positive or negative, without knowledge or examination of the facts, you are being prejudiced. Whenever you come up with some preconceived notion based on things such as race, color, political alignment, or even the way people dress, it taints your ability to accurately read others. Our prejudices can be based on our fears, feeling threatened, upbringing or a myriad of other things.

There are many other specific techniques used in learning how to understand people better, but for the purposes of creating community, knowing that we will be much more effective leaders when we share more of ourselves and let go of our own prejudices in order to truly see the other person, is enough. We can't expect others to get excited about creating community and learn about their motivations if we don't share with them what makes us excited about it, and we won't get much support or participation if we make invalid assumptions about others based upon our own personal prejudices. It's as simple as that.

Exercise: During your day, take notice of your interactions with others and how many layers of ourselves we reveal to those we come in contact with. Then, notice the corresponding layer of others that are revealed to you. When you increase the depth of your interaction and share more, is there a corresponding increase in the depth of their sharing?

Remember, the purpose of learning the fundamentals of understanding someone better are to become more effective at understanding the motivations of others so that you can provide them with acceptable opportunities to become involved. Trying to invite the owner who complained about cleaning up after dogs to join the social committee may not be acceptable, unless during a conversation you shared enough of yourself to get the person to confide that they would like to meet more people in the community and maybe help plan social events. When you risk true engagement with others, anything is possible. As a leader, engagement is a powerful tool and can be used more effectively when you understand the dynamics involved in getting others to open up . . . like an onion!

The Five Most Important Leadership Traits

Some sit and pontificate about whether leaders are made or born. The genuine leader ignores such arguments and instead concentrates on developing the leadership qualities necessary for success. Here, we are going to discuss five leadership traits or leadership qualities that people look for in a leader. If you are able to increase your skill in displaying these five quality characteristics, you will make it easier for people to want to join in the community building effort.

The five leadership traits/leadership qualities are:

1. **Honest**
2. **Forward-Looking**
3. **Competent**

4. **Inspiring**
5. **Intelligent**

These five qualities come from Kouzes and Posner's research into leadership that was done for the book *The Leadership Challenge*.

Your skill at exhibiting these five leadership qualities is strongly correlated with people's desire to follow your lead. Exhibiting these traits will inspire confidence in your leadership. Not exhibiting these traits or exhibiting the opposite of these traits will decrease your leadership influence with those around you.

It is important to exhibit, model and display these traits. Simply possessing each trait is not enough; you have to display it in a way that people notice. People want to see that you actively demonstrate these leadership qualities and will not just assume that you have them. It isn't enough to just be neutral. For example, just because you are not dishonest will not cause people to recognize that you are honest. Just avoiding displays of incompetence won't inspire the same confidence as truly displaying competence.

The focus of each of these five traits needs to be on what people see you do—not just the things they don't see you do, which is what we have concentrated on so far. Being honest isn't a matter of not lying—it is taking the extra effort to display honesty.

Honesty as a Leadership Quality: *People want to follow an honest leader. Years ago, many people started out by assuming that their leadership was honest simply because the authority of their position. With modern scandals, this is no longer true.*

When you assume a leadership position, you need to understand that people will think you are a little dishonest. *In order to be seen as an honest individual, you will have to go out of your way to display honesty.* People will not assume you are honest simply because you have never been caught lying.

One of the most frequent places where leaders miss an opportunity to display honesty is in handling mistakes. Much of a leader's job is to try new things and refine the ideas that don't work. However, many leaders want to avoid failure to the extent that they don't admit when something did not work. In creating community, we are working in areas that have, up until now, been undefined and as such, mistakes will occur.

For example, a board decides to add an additional feature to their community website. This feature would allow owners to post comments about the community so that other owners could reply and respond. It didn't take long for the board to realize that this new feature was creating a lot of disharmony within the association because those few owners who held extremely negative perceptions of the community association were monopolizing the posts with complaints and insults about the board, management, neighbors and the community in general.

The board reviewed what was happening and realized that this new website feature was doing the opposite of what it was intended to do. Instead of uniting owners through constructive dialogue and ideas, it was further dividing owners as many felt that they were under attack by the few negative owners or began to believe that the community was indeed as misguided as the posts indicated. The board discontinued the feature and included a detailed explanation as to why it was discontinued and that they would look at other possibilities to help owners unite in a more positive environment. *When mistakes do happen, consider them a chance for the board to display honesty with the owners, be candid about why things didn't work out as expected, learn from the mistakes and move on.*

Opportunities to display honesty on a large scale may not happen every day. As a leader, showing people that you are honest even when it means admitting to a mistake, displays a key trait that people are looking for in their leaders. By demonstrating honesty with yourself, with your community and with outside organizations, you will increase your leadership influence. People will trust someone who actively displays honesty—not just as an honest individual, but as someone who is worth following.

Forward-Looking as a Leadership Trait: The whole point of leadership is figuring out where to go from where you are now. While you may know where you want to go, people won't see that unless you actively communicate it with them. Remember, these traits aren't just things you need to have, they are things you need to actively display to those around you.

When people do not consider their leader forward-looking, that leader is usually suffering from one of two possible problems:

1. The leader doesn't have a forward-looking vision.
2. The leader is unwilling or scared to share the vision with others.

When a leader doesn't have a vision for the future, it usually because they are spending so much time on today, that they haven't really thought about tomorrow. On a very simplistic level this can be solved simply by setting aside some time for planning, strategizing and thinking about the future.

Many times when a leader has no time to think and plan for the future, it is because they are doing a poor job of leading in the present. They have created a leadership systems that relies too much on the leader for input at every stage.

Some leaders have a clear vision, but don't wish to share it with others. Most of the time they are concerned that they will lose credibility if they share a vision of the future that doesn't come about. This is a legitimate concern. However, people need to know that a leader has a strong vision for the future and a strong plan for going forward. Leaders run into trouble sharing their vision of the future when they start making promises to individuals. This goes back to the trait of honesty. If a board member tells an owner that "next year I'm going to make you chairman of the landscape committee" that may be a promise they can't keep. The leader is probably basing this promise on the assumption that the current chairman is not interested in keeping the position the following year and if they do and have done an outstanding job, it makes no sense to make the change, but the owner will only hear the personal promise.

Leaders can communicate their goals and vision for the future without making promises that they may not be able to keep. If a leader needs to make a promise to an individual, it should be tied to certain measurable objectives or situations being met.

Competency as a Leadership Quality: People want to follow someone who is competent. This doesn't mean a leader needs to be the foremost expert on every area of the entire affairs of the community association, but they need to be able to demonstrate competency.

For a leader to demonstrate that they are competent, it isn't enough to just avoid displaying incompetency. Some people will assume you are competent because of your leadership position, but most will have to see demonstrations before deciding that you are competent.

When people under your leadership look at some action you have taken and think, "that just goes to show why he is the one in charge", you are demonstrating competency. If these moments are infrequent, it is likely that some demonstrations of competency will help boost your leadership influence.

Like the other traits, it isn't enough for a leader to be competent. They must demonstrate competency in a way that people notice. This can be a delicate balance. There is a danger of drawing too much attention to yourself in a way that makes the leader seem arrogant. Another potential danger is that of minimizing others contributions and appearing to take credit for the work of others.

As a leader, one of the safest ways to "toot you own horn without blowing it", is to celebrate and bring attention to community achievements. In this way you indirectly point out your competency as a leader. For example: "Last year I set a goal of fully-funding the reserves and, thanks to everyone's hard work, as of today, we have reached fully-funded levels."

Inspiration as a Leadership Trait: *People want to be inspired. In fact, there is a whole class of people who will follow an inspiring leader—even when the leader has no other qualities. If you have developed the other traits we have already discussed, being inspiring is usually just a matter of communicating clearly and with passion. Being inspiring means telling people how your community association is going to change their lives.*

A great example of inspiration is when Steve Jobs stole the CEO from Pepsi by asking him, "Do you want to sell sugar water for the rest of your life, or do you want to change the world?" This example may be a bit 'over the top' for a community association, but *being inspiring means showing people the big picture and helping them see beyond a narrow focus and understand how their part fits into the big picture.*

One technique to develop your ability to inspire is telling stories. Stories can be examples from your experience, fictitious examples told to you by others, or even historical fables and myths. Stories can help you vividly illustrate what you are trying to communicate. Stories that communicate on an emotional level help communicate deeper than words and leave an imprint much stronger than anything you can achieve through a simple stating of the facts.

Learning to be inspiring is not easy, particularly for individuals lacking in charisma. It can be learned. Take note of people who inspire you and analyze the way they communicate. Look for ways to passionately express your vision. While there will always be room for improvement, a small investment in effort and awareness will give you a significant improvement in this leadership trait.

Intelligence as a Leadership Trait*: Intelligence is something that can be difficult to develop. The road toward becoming more intelligent is difficult, long and can't be completed without investing considerable time. Developing intelligence is a lifestyle choice. Your college graduation was the beginning of your education, not the end. In fact, much of what is taught in college functions merely as a foundational language for lifelong educational experiences.*

To develop intelligence you need to commit to continual learning, both formally and informally. The Community Association Institute offers classes for community leaders and have chapters in most of the larger areas of the country.

Informally, you can develop a great deal of intelligence in any field simply by investing a reasonable amount of time to reading on a daily basis. The fact is that most people won't make a regular investment in their education. *Spending 30 minutes of focused reading every day will give you 182 hours of study time each year.*

For the most part, people will notice if you are intelligent by observing your behavior and attitude. Trying to display your intelligence is likely to be counterproductive. One of the greatest signs of someone who is truly intelligent is humility. The greater your education, the greater your understanding of how little we really understand.

You can demonstrate your intelligence by gently leading people toward understanding, even when you know the answer. Your focus needs to be on helping others learn, not demonstrating how smart you are. Arrogance will put you in a position where people are secretly hopeful that you'll make a mistake and appear foolish.

As unintuitive as it may seem, one of the best ways to exhibit intelligence is by asking questions. *Learning from the people you lead by asking thoughtful questions will do more to enhance your intelligence credibility than just about anything.* Of course this means you need to be capable of asking intelligent questions.

People like to consider themselves to be intelligent and interesting. If you ask someone to talk about an area of their expertise and spend the time to really understand what they are saying (as demonstrated by asking questions) their opinion of your intelligence will go up. After all, you now know more about what makes them so intelligent, so you must be smart as well. Your ability to demonstrate respect for the intellect of others will probably do more to influence the perception of your intellect than your actual intelligence.

Summary of the Five Leadership Qualities: *By consciously making an effort to exhibit these traits, people will be more likely to follow you. These are the most important traits that people look for in their leaders. By exhibiting them on a regular basis, you will be able to grow your influence to its potential as a leader.*

Embracing New Leadership: Apprenticeship

The concept of serving an apprenticeship in order to learn a new trade or skill is centuries old. Though it is quickly going out of date with the advancements in technology and learning, apprenticeship should be embraced by community association leaders in order to cultivate tomorrow's leaders. The political activist and four-time Presidential candidate, Ralph Nader, advises, ". . . start with the premise that the function of leadership is to produce more leaders, not more followers."

The owner who chooses to read the community newsletter or visit the community website today is the board member of tomorrow. Owners who serve on committees, volunteer to help at social events or go door-to-door in order to collect proxy votes in order to obtain quorum for the annual meeting, are all prospective community association leaders. Identifying them and grooming them to take your place not only ensures that current community building efforts continue, but that future community association leaders are competent and willing to serve the best interests of the entire community.

One of the reasons that there is not more turnover on the board of directors is that there are not enough owners willing to volunteer their time to serve on the board. Thus, in a sense, the current board becomes kidnapped by the apathetic community owners and the ransom is another term—or three—serving on the board of directors. Not exactly the ideal scenario to help create community because, for the most part, those kidnapped board members lack the enthusiasm and patience required in order to implement new ideas and provide direction to promote unity. Their goal becomes just to survive their time on the board, obtain their release and get on with their lives. This scenario is a very common one, but hopefully, if many of the community building ideas and techniques suggested along our journey together are embraced and used, can be avoided in the future. Genuine leadership has to take in account the vacuum of leadership that will exist once they leave their positions in the community association and address that inevitability long before they leave that position. Taking other owners 'under their wing' and sharing with them some of the subtle and not-so-subtle secrets of effective community association leadership over a prolonged period of time is how that is accomplished. We will call it a program of community association leader apprenticeship.

It is also very common that many of the owners who choose to pursue leadership positions within a community association come from a background of private business leadership. Their experiences as a business owner or manager appear to be a perfect fit for community association leadership and most owners, if given the choice, would probably pick someone who ran a bank over someone who taught third grade when selecting leadership for their community. This way of thinking could be a big mistake. With little or no previous experience in community association leadership, the banker is most likely to employ management strategies that have worked for them in business. The challenge is that those that they lead in the business world are getting paid to work for them and are obligated to perform their duties to the satisfaction of the employer or risk losing their job and their livelihood. In the world of community association leadership, the people who the leader serves are doing so as volunteers and out of a sense of service to others. Leadership strategies that are successful in private business often do not translate into successful leadership strategies in the community association environment because if a volunteer does not perform to the leader's expectations (which are much higher because of their previous experience in business and the standard expected from paid employees) then the volunteer can just quit and will suffer nothing more than creating additional free time in their life.

The third grade teacher, on the other hand, is skilled in patience, listening, teaching and reinforcing positive behaviors. The world of the teacher is one of contribution to the betterment of future society. Their successes are not measured in profit or loss or by bank balance, but by the successes of their students. Those qualities fit much more naturally into the dynamics of successful community association leadership than those of a banker because the qualities of a teacher speak to the needs of creating community more effectively. The community association is a not-for-profit corporation that is driven by volunteers not money. Patience, the ability to listen, the gift of helping others learn and being comfortable rewarding others for their good work is the currency of success for a community association, not dollars.

Creating a leadership apprenticeship program—whether formal or simply as a goal of the board's mission statement—allows anyone an opportunity to adjust their leadership styles accordingly so that they work in the community association arena far ahead of the time when they actually take a leadership position. It eliminates, or at least drastically reduces, the dreaded downward learning curve that changes in leadership usually create within the community. This downward learning curve usually comes at the expense of other volunteer leaders, owners, association management company representatives and/or service providers who have to adjust to new ways of doing things and continues until effective changes are made to the leadership style or the new leader is the only one left standing.

How does one go about establishing an apprenticeship program in order to groom future community association leaders? The same way that all real progress needs to be achieved in an association that is on the road to community, by committee. The board of directors can create a leadership committee whose function would be to solicit potential community leaders and offer them opportunities to participate in educational opportunities in order to learn about the roles of the various positions of leadership, how management functions and in-depth exposure to the governing documents and state law. Some management companies offer orientation programs that touch on these topics and the Community Associations Institute (CAI) also has classes available.

Members of the leadership committee would attend board meetings, be given committee responsibilities and be asked to provide valuable input when brainstorming ideas or establishing the mission statement for the board or the charters for committees. Being on the leadership committee should be considered a privilege and it should be well known throughout the community that its members are being groomed for community association leadership positions. Although members of this committee are solicited or recommended by the board or committee chairs or other owners, anyone who expresses a sincere desire to be a part of it should be given that opportunity.

Supervision and coordination of the leadership committee should come from the most effective board members and committee chairs. Because many of the previous community building components we have already discussed should be in place, an environment of community, unity, shared responsibility and goodwill should already have roots in the leadership process. This means there is more interest and, more importantly, more participation in every aspect of the community association management process and that means more support for current and future leadership.

Trying to establish a leadership committee before any progress is made in creating community would be a mistake because until there is effective leadership committed to, and working towards, a greater sense of community consciousness, the lessons being taught future leaders may only reinforce old, dysfunctional leadership styles. If that were to happen, no matter how much progress is made in creating community—and we can assume not much since the level of community consciousness would still at the embryonic stage—when it is time for the new leaders to take over, everything will have to begin again. Creating

It is important to remember, as was mentioned in the previous chapter on the faces of empowerment, that community building is a developmental process and is done in stages. The establishment of an effective leadership committee should take place once there is a cohesive board working together with established committees and owner interest and participation has increased in order to warrant energy being spent on the long-term plans for establishing future leaders. Simply put, there has to be a pool of potential future leaders in which to draw from, otherwise the current leaders will end up being the future leaders . . . again.

Given the emerging nature of community consciousness within the association, if there were enough interest, the board could create an educational committee whose main purpose is to provide the curriculum, if you will, that the leadership committee would follow until their opportunity to either being appointed to committee chair positions or run for election to the board of directors arises. Personally, I like the idea of an educational committee because they could also be responsible for other facets of community learning such as:

- *Owner orientations: Owners learn the leader's roles and responsibilities and their own responsibilities as owners are reinforced: compliance, participation, voting, etc.*
- *Board orientations: Board members are introduced to community building philosophy and begin the process of brainstorming, creating a map to follow for the coming year and revisiting and/or establishing an effective mission statement.*
- *Committee orientations: Committee chairs and members meet in order to establish goals and objectives of each committee*

and how they effectively interface with the board of directors and management.

- **Management orientations**: *If self-managed, upon change of manager, an introduction into the culture of the community association and expectations and responsibilities of management. If managed by a management company, the same introduction as above in addition to how the management company's services can effectively compliment the work of the association (a novel concept considering management companies tend to work in the opposite direction).*

- **Service provider orientations**: *Community service vendors are introduced to the culture of the community and the expectations expected of them. In addition, the service providers are given the opportunity to share their operating procedures and how best the association can utilize their services.*

Whether a leadership committee or an educational committee, when helping others learn it is important to utilize the correct use of instructive strategies, or as <u>Paulo Freire</u>, the reknowned Brazillian educator, referred to as "<u>critical pedagogy</u>," a method of teaching adults (as opposed to children, who learn in different stages than adults do). Freire promoted the use of cooperation, unity, and organization (dialogics) in helping to empower others through education.

<u>Malcolm Knowles</u>, an American adult educator, reasoned that the term <u>andragogy</u> (Greek: "man-leading") is more pertinent when discussing adult learning and teaching than the more commonly used <u>pedagogy</u> (Greek: "child-leading") used by Freire. He referred to andragogy as the art and science of teaching adults.

Knowles' theory can be stated with six assumptions related to <u>motivation</u> of adult learning:

1. Adults need to know the reason for learning something (Need to Know)
2. Experience (including error) provides the basis for learning activities (Foundation).
3. Adults need to be responsible for their decisions on education; involvement in the planning and evaluation of their instruction (Self-concept).
4. Adults are most interested in learning subjects having immediate relevance to their work and/or personal lives (Readiness).
5. Adult learning is problem-centered rather than content-oriented (Orientation).
6. Adults respond better to internal versus external motivators (Motivation).

The term, andragogy, has been used by some to allow discussion of contrast between self-directed and 'taught' education. When used in conjunction with Freire's theories about cooperation, unity and organization, both learning systems compliment each other perfectly when helping to empower community association owners through education. I understand that neither model has been given its due here, but my hope is to introduce you to the basic tenents of each system. Either model of learning is worth looking at in more detail if the community association is serious about embracing the role of educating those that live in and work with the community. As with most community building activities, educating owners is not a legally mandated duty of the board of directors, but certainly enhances the effectiveness of meeting those responsibilities (to preserve, protect and enhance the common assets of the association).

Conclusion

Leadership is the rudder that steers the community association towards its goal of creating community. Becoming an effective leader is an acquired skill and along with following legally mandated duties, an important factor in being an effective leader requires creative responses to solving community challenges and an active and conscious effort to groom other community owners to replace them when their leadership time is up. With strong, present and proactive leadership in place that recognizes that their greatest asset are the members of the community and that all the good things that happen on the road to creating community are due to their involvement, the potiential to improve the quality of everyone's life in the community is unlimited.

Because our goal has always been the empowerment of all community members (which creates the framework of community), it is through the attitudes and actions of the community leadership that empowerment is possible. Getting everyone's attention, encouraging positive feedback, welcoming all forms of participation and utilizing the work of engaged committees defines great community association leadership. Hopefully, by this point, you are starting to realize creating community is not an impossible task, but is the result of looking at the challenge in a new way and following a logical progression of community building steps, each of which takes us one step closer to personal empowerment and an increased sense of unity in the community.

In the next chapter, we will explore an example of a community association that has embraced the principles we have been discussing and created an environment that is the model for creating community.

IT'S A COMMUNITY

Attachment and Empowerment

*All happy families are alike; each unhappy family is unhappy
in its own way.*

Leo Tolstoy, <u>Anna Karenina</u>

We have reached the final steps of our journey and can actually see the promised land in the distance: community. As we end our time together, keep in mind that as you look at your community, the names and the forms of the community building tools that each association needs to embrace in order to create community consciousness are far less important than their meaning or purpose. Each community will evolve and adapt the community building tools that will work best for it and not every tool is appropriate for every community. Some community associations will reach community with only an engaged board of directors leading the way. Their sense of unity established through more informal group activities that feed each owner's individual need for belonging and attachment. Other communities will achieve unity through a dozen active and involved formal committees assisting the board as they govern the community and begin to grow community consciousness. The forms are different but the meaning, their common *alikeness*, is the same for both: to bring about unity and foster a *sense of attachment* to the community. When residents unite and feel more attached to their community, they are more likely to be involved and their life and the lives of everyone in it are improved. *Community elevates everyone within it and it gives people something to live for instead of just someplace to live.* Increase the attachment that people have in their community and there is unity. Empower a group of unified residents and you have community in the truest sense of the word.

What Attaches People to Their Communities?

What makes a community a desirable place to live and contribute their attention to? What draws people to stake their future in it? Are communities with more attached residents better off?

Gallup and the John S. and James L. Knight Foundation launched the Knight Soul of the Community (SOTC) project in 2008 with these questions in mind. The study focuses on the emotional side of the connection between residents and their communities. They studied 10 domains that were found to drive community attachment at varying levels:

- Basic services—community infrastructure
- Economic conditions
- Safety
- Leadership
- Aesthetics—physical beauty and green spaces
- Education systems
- Social offerings—opportunities for social interaction and citizen caring
- Openness/welcomeness—how welcoming the community is to different people
- Involvement—residents' commitment to their community through voting or volunteerism
- Social capital—social networks between residents

After interviewing close to 43,000 people in 26 communities over three years, the study found that three main qualities (drivers) attach people to place: **social offerings** (events, places to meet), **openness** (how welcoming a place is) and the community's **aesthetics** (its physical beauty and green spaces). After three years of research, the results have been very consistent, and surprising.

First, what attaches residents to their communities doesn't change much from place to place. While we might expect that the drivers of attachment would be different in Miami, Fla., from those in Long Beach, CA., in fact, the main drivers of attachment show little difference across communities. In addition, the same drivers have risen to the top in every year of the study (2008/2009/2010).

Second, these main drivers may be surprising. While economic conditions are obviously the subject of much attention, the study has found that perceptions of the community's economic condition do not have a very strong relationship to resident attachment. Instead, attachment is most closely related to how accepting a community is of diversity, its wealth of social offerings, and its aesthetics.

And finally, while they did see differences in attachment among different demographic groups, demographics generally are not the strongest drivers of attachment. In almost every community, they found that a resident's perceptions of the community are more strongly linked to their level of community attachment than to that person's age, ethnicity, work status, etc.

What this means to us is that we will have a better chance of creating community when community leaders use the SOTC study's findings to maximize community strengths and address challenge areas to improve community attachment. For example; organizing regular social events, reaching out to all residents and maintaining the aesthetic beauty of the community all contribute mightily to creating community. Let's look at these drivers in more detail.

Social Offerings: If your community has a clubhouse, use it. If it doesn't, find another location within the community in which to hold regular social functions, such as the pool area, a greenbelt area, a cul-de-sac or a park. Those communities with a clubhouse are at a definate advantage because there are so many social opportunities available just because of having a place to go that is not outside—and subject to the weather—that can accommodate many people. However, that doesn't mean that if your community doesn't have a clubhouse that you can't think out-of-the-box and still plan great social events. Community movie night, exercise classes, bunko, potlucks and other social events can be held out in a greenbelt area just as easily as a clubhouse, they are just dependent upon good weather.

One of the best motivators to encourage attendance and participation at annual meetings is to coordinate it in conjunction with a community social event. I've worked with community associations that have rented inflatable jumpers for the kids, purchased hot dogs and hamburgers for barbecue, organized community parades and held organized games. Then, in the middle of the social event, an annual meeting breaks out! Brillant! I've also worked with numerous community associations who do nothing other than send out annual meeting notices and can never obtain quorums due to a lack of participation by owners. They schedule one adjourned annual meeting after another until either a lower quorum number kicks in due to a governing document stipulation or the board just decides to give up and stays on board for another year. One would think that after the first year that quorum could not be achieved on the first try that another approach would be in order. If you always do what you always did, you'll always get what you always got.

I recommend a quarterly schedule of large-scale community events in order to satisfy the social offering driver needed for community attachment. Consider a spring social event, a summer barbecue, a fall harvest festival and a holiday party, for example. Surely one of these events can be coordinated during the time the annual meeting is to be held. Volunteers (members of the social committee) can go out into the surrounding business community and solicit donations of food and prizes (the prized to be raffled off) in exchange for sponsorship advertising or just goodwill. There really is no reason that this approach should not be considered by every community association, regardless of size. The only reason that I can think of is that the leadership either doesn't think anyone will show up or they don't have the resources (time, energy, funds, volunteers) to pull them off.

What that kind of an attitude says to me is that the problem is not that the residents won't show up or that the resources don't exist, the problem is that leadership doesn't understand the importance of social events in running the association. I can see the heads shaking now and the comments about social events having nothing to do with protecting, preserving and enhancing the common assets of the community. Reserve funding, assessment collection, rule compliance and tree trimming, now those are some issues that are appropriate for a board of directors to deal with, not inflatable jumpers!

The only flaw in that logic is that every one of those "appropriate" issues demand the involvement and participation of the residents if they are to be successful. If the key to increased involvment and participation is to help residents feel as if they are truly part of the community (attached) and share common perceptions about their community (unity), then shouldn't the board utilize the most effective tools at their disposal to accomplish the task of increasing involvment and participation?

I've tried to share numerous tools that have been shown to be effective in bringing people together. None of them require anything more than a willingness, on the side of the community leaders, to look at the relationship with their community members differently and risk making changes that will aim to empower everyone in the community. Following the letter of the law (protecting, preserving and enhancing the common assets) is best accomplished through the spirit of community . . . and sometimes the spirit of community demands inflatable jumpers!

Openness: How accepting a community is of diversity is communicated through an attitude of welcoming and corresponding actions that reinforce that attitude. Everyone must feel as if they are invited to the community building party. It goes back to the attitude of inclusion versus exclusion, the effective use of communication tools in order to reinforce the 'invitation' and providing everyone an opportunity to contribute. If, for any reason, community association leaders think along the lines of, "we want some participation, but we don't want everyone to get involved" then we do not have openness. A good exercise to determine just how 'open' you are is to finish this sentence: "Of all the various groups of people, the ones that I would least like to have as a neighbor are . . ."

The answer(s) to that question reveal a lot about your acceptence of diversity. If you don't have any real issues with most people being your neighbor, then your lack of judgemental prejudices informs your sense of welcoming and you make everyone feel as if they belong around you. The group leadership dynamic is not so easy to decipher because the more people involved the more opportunities there are for past experiences, cultural upbringing, and personal biases to come into play. To avoid challenges with openness, community association leadership should establish a firm and committed consensus that not only is everyone in the community invited to the party, but that the invitation is stated over and over again in their actions and communications with the residents.

Aesthetics: Living in an attractive environment creates a strong emotional attachment to the community and is shared by everyone who lives there. It is a powerful point of unity and can not be underestimated when creating community. We've discussed the effective use of committees, board priorities and effective communication in order to get others to contribute to keeping the community looking its best, but the best way is unite others in that pursuit is to ensure that the community's curb appeal and landscape maintenance is high on the list of community association leadership priorities. For most board members, this is probably the easiest task to accomplish when creating community because it is one of the easiest to measure. Just look around.

When there is litter in the common areas, dog poop in the pool area, garage doors that are faded and in dire need of maintenance, weeds in the flower beds and mailboxes that are falling apart, then I can guarantee you that the environment is working against you in your efforts to create community. In a sense, you can tell a lot about how effective a community association is led by how it looks. For some community associations that have suffered from a lack of engaged and effective leadership, one of the first things that should be done in order to change direction and begin building community consciousness is to clean up the community.

By focusing on those issues that are association responsibilities first (greenbelts, gardens, pool area, etc.) leadership is setting an example and as the community begins to look better, people will begin to take notice. Then, shifting to owner-responsible maintenance items won't be so difficult. It's hard to get owners to paint their garage doors when the rest of the community looks shabby. It's much easier when their faded garage door sticks out like a sore thumb compared to the rest of the community. Again, its all about motivation and how to use it.

Final thoughts on what attaches people to their communities: At this point in our journey, everything should be coming together to illustrate just how important it is to transcend our limited way of thinking about our community association and embrace the possibility that creating community is far more about affect then it is about effect. The best ways to create (effect) community is by understanding the origins of community consciousness (affect) that motivates the community residents to wake up, take notice and come to the party. Along with empowerment, it's about giving them opportunities to come together, feel welcomed and appreciated, and enjoy the beauty of their community.

Achieving Empowerment

Now, let's wrap this party up and finish it off with a more detailed conversation about the three components of empowerment that creating community is based upon. Much of what has been presented thus far is the philosophical foundation that must be poured before we can build community upon it. When we truly understand the dynamics of empowerment, it will become second nature and everything you do will be a reflection of that understanding. When you empower others, creating community becomes inevitable and will surround you no matter where you are.

The three components of empowerment are:
1. **Find out what people are thinking and what they believe the problems are**
2. **Let them design the solutions**
3. **Get out of the way and let them put those solutions into practice**

Empowerment demands that all three of its components be addressed and implemented in order to be truly effective.

Find out what people are thinking and what they believe the problems are: In order to find out what people are thinking and what they believe the problems in your community are, you have to ask them. Which means you have to make a connection with them, hold a conversation with them and listen to them. As simple as that sounds, how does one go about accomplishing that, in say, a community association of 700 homes? If your community has only 15 homes, one could easily go door-to-door and in a few evenings accomplish the task. But with 700 homes, the job is much more difficult, especially if a majority of those residents are not engaged with or interested in their community association. "I pay my dues and obey the rules. So, don't bother me!" are common sentitments, even if only unconsciously expressed in their lack of interest or participation in their community.

In a community where disinterest is the norm, annual meeting quorums are usually difficult to obtain. That should be a sign that mailed or website surveys, in order to find out what people are thinking or what they think the problems are, will probably go unanswered. That doesn't mean to not use surveys, what that means is that you will have to address the challenge from more than one angle. There SHOULD be more than one way to encourage people to share their thoughts with you. Remember, understanding what people think is a necessary step that needs to happen in order for empowerment to be achieved AND maintained. You can't just try to get people to share with you, you have to succeed at it . . . over and over and over again. In creating community it is a never ending process and if understood in that light, makes the challenge much easier because it should put community association leaders in a constant state of mind to look for listening opportunities.

Surveys (mailed or posted on the website) are always great and should always be available and used. However, in the beginning of creating community consciousness, more informal methods may be more effective. Planning social gatherings where people are more likely to open up about their feelings are extremely effective if leadership consciously uses those opportunities to encourage the sharing of thoughts and ideas. *Walking the neighborhood and talking to neighbors and letting them know leadership wants community input is a great way to spread the word. Newsletter articles, website updates and email alerts that explain specific issues and ask for input should always augment the listening process.* Neighborhood watch programs divide the community up into manageable areas and create block captains who can be asked to help obtain feedback from those residents in their area of responsibility.

Once there is a recognized environment created that encourages resident input, ideas, suggestions, concerns and even complaints, then more formal means—such as surveys—will always be more successful because residents understand that leadership really is interested in what they have to say. Getting to that point is going to take time though because it probably requires a culture change within leadership. Going from non-receptive or neutrally-receptive leadership to a fully-engaged, receptive leadership culture takes time to evolve and become recognized by the residents. For example, once residents realize that their comments to leadership about lighting at the front entrance monument are taken seriously and, more importantly, acted upon, they are more likely to expand their willlingness to share their thoughts and ideas with leadership.

It is vitally important to remember for those community associations that are professionally managed that almost every attempt to solicit input from the residents will go through management. So, management has to be just as committed to the process of creating community as the board of directors is. If they are not, it will never happen. This is an extremely important point so I want to repeat it: *Management has to be just as committed to the process of creating community as the board of directors is.* If they are not, it will never happen. Why? Because management should be the hub of communication for the community association. All communication—coming in and going out—should be done through management. If it isn't, then I hope it is by design because coordinating communication is one of the most important functions of professional management. If the management company representative does not understand the value of proactive communication or how it enhances their client's success at community building (and their own efforts at effective time management), then all the community building concepts, ideas, methods and strategies presented in this book will just be seen as "another thing they don't have time to do" by the manager. My first book, *Taking Control—Time Management and Communication Tools for Community Association Management*, addresses that issue in depth so I won't dwell on that dynamic here, but suffice it to say that management will play a key role in the success or failure of creating community so make sure leadership and management are on the same page when creating community.

If I've done my job thus far and effectively conveyed the fundamentals of creating community, coming up with ideas that will motivate owners to begin constructive communication with management should not be difficult. As I've mentioned before, each community has its own personality and there are different specific motivators that will work for one community that may not work for another. That said, here are some additional motivational ideas on where/how to get people to share what they are thinking and what they believe the problems are with their community association:

- Surveys (newsletter/mail/online/email)
- Online reporting/comment forms
- Door-to-door canvassing
- Social events
- Community programs (i.e., neighborhood watch)
- Annual meeting discussions
- Open forum participation
- Management tracking phone calls/correspondence
- Committee questionnaires

- Informal town hall meetings
- Resident brainstorming sessions
- Landscape/maintenance walk-throughs
- Suggestion box posted in common area
- Discussions with neighbors
- Telephone surveys
- Community improvement idea contest

Once in a while a community challenge will be identified by a resident that the board and management are unaware of, but most of the problems identified by residents will not be surprises to leadership. In fact, the community leaders probably could have come up with the same problems on their own without resident input. However, not utilizing resident input undermines the whole purpose of empowering residents and creating community. It is also one of the reasons why many boards do not do more to solicit resident input regarding community problems. It takes more time, effort and energy to try to get owners to wake up, take notice and get involved. If the board can identify the same issues, then why bother?. But, since community consciousness demands involvment, it is a step that must be taken in order to create community. It is the process that matters, not the product.

The power of addressing resident identified issues lies in the fact that leadership is acknowledging the influence of the owners. That acknowlegement speaks volumes about the how the residents will perceive leadership and leadership's commitment to the importance of resident participation. It sets the tone for all the other elements of creating community consciousness and empowerment.

Let them design the solutions: Once residents become open to communicating with leadership/management, the second step of empowerment is to provide them with the opportunity to solve the problems that they identified. From a community association dynamic, the only real effective way to accomplish this step is through the work of committees. We have already spent a considerable amount of time on the use and benefits of committee work, so we will focus here on the transition from listening to residents and identifying community challenges to turning over those challenges to committees in order for them to design the solutions that will best address those challenges.

Keep in mind that both the listening to residents and allowing them to design the solutions to identified problems is an ongoing process. The tools that motivate residents to share their thoughts should not be discontinued just because leadership feels that there is enough on the community's plate to deal with and decides to stop encouraging input for a while in order to deal with those problems. Once started, the community building process should be like a runaway train on an endless track going in the direction of community.

Whether at the beginning of the community building process or somewhere in the middle, the abililty of the leaders to assign specific problems to specific committees is at the heart of empowerment and creating community. If a problem is identified that does not have an established standing or ad-hoc committee to turn the solution-finding process over to, then create one. *Those same residents that helped identify the problem are the ideal members to serve on that committee.* Not all will, but even a committee of two will create more opportunities for empowerment than no committee at all.

The goals of empowerment for the community and how those goals are to be achieved should be established at the onset of the board's shift to community building strategies. You don't want to establish programs and utilize community building tools on the sly and then one day announce to the owners that they are suddenly a real community. It doesn't and can't work that way. Remember our conversation about transparency? Leadership's decisions and goals for creating community must be just as transparent as their decision to rennovate the front entrance momument or pass a special assessment to maintain a capital asset of the community association.

When community challenges are assigned to committees and the committees begin the task of designing solutions to solve those challenges, be sure that those committees utilize all the resources at their disposal. If professionally managed, the management company has access to considerable clout and professional connections that can be used during the research stage of problem solving. Community service providers and neighbors with experience in the area that is being addressed may also be a great resource. It takes input from others both inside and outside of the community in order to determine the best course of action to suggest to the board. If the issue concerns the pool area, asking the pool service company for input should be first on the 'to do' list. If the issue is with slope maintenance or landscaping, then the landscape company should be solicited for input. It will be up to each individual committee to determine how they want to research possible solutions, but if the challenge is complex, the one thing they shouldn't do is to simply sit together in a room and try to think of solutions on their own without professional input. They may be able to come to similar conclusions as the professionals, however the recommendations that they make to the board should be based on the best options available at the time. That requires obtaining the best professional opinions in order to bolster and reinforce their recommendations. If bids are required to be solicited, then the committees need to work closely with management in order to ensure that all bids obtained are based upon the same specifications.

Get out of the way and let them put those solutions into practice: Assuming that the residents are identifying the challenges that exist within the community and the committees are functioning and resarching and recommending solutions to those challenges, then all that is left is for leadership to work with those recommendations and begin bringing the vision of the committee to life. Simple as that.

If the first two steps of empowerment are carried out and leadership does not act on the recommendations, they better have a pretty good reason. Without a good reason not to consider the committee's recommendations, it could undermine any community building accomplished thus far, especially if there is a long-suffering pattern of ignoring committee work by the board. In those instances, sometimes it is a lack of working perameters established by the board that results in some boards ignoring the hard work done by the committees. The committees simply do more than they were expected to. The solution to that is for leadership to be clear with the committees as to what is expected of them. Sometimes, the committees have a much wider range of vision than the board and see their work from a much broader perspective. Again, clarity is the solution.

I know of a large community association that had a fairly vital committee system in place. However, no matter how complete and detailed the committee's recommendations to the board were, the board always seemed to find some reason to shoot down the committee's work. When the board couldn't find a reason to ignore the recommendations, they would postpone approval and cite 'further research needed' in the minutes and have management table discussion on the recommendations until a future meeting. It didn't take long for the community volunteers to realize they were wasting their time and the committee system fell apart. The board had used the committee structure in order to keep the residents occupied and out of their way and never had any intention of implementing any of the committees suggestions. When confronted, the board president stated that most of the committee recommendations would have required an increase in assessments and that the board's number one priority was to keep assessments as low as possible. As of this writing the owners are working to unseat the current board and are working to restore the community consciousness that leadership had undermined by failing to be clear with the committees about how they would measure their recommendations.

A cautionary note is in order at this point. Keep in mind that creating community is a developing process that unfolds in stages. Just as the earlier chapters dealt with various stages and elements of community building, so does this one. The period of time between the first stage of empowerment and the second stage could be months or it could be years. It all depends upon the foundations of community that are laid down beforehand. It is human tendency to forget that and when reading about these three stages of empowerment, a typical response might be something akin to skepticism because they have never experienced it before. For those readers whose community's leadership struggle with apathy, disinterest and owners unwilling to volunteer, the movement from that reality to one in which committees are suppose to work out all the solutions to the community's woes is an enormous amount of change to accept. At the beginning of our journey together I asked for you to suspend your pessimism about creating community and remain open to think about community in a new way. We have covered a lot of ground in these pages together and it is highly unlikely that you have taken the 'cookbook' method of creating community: implementing each suggestion one at a time, waiting for a result and then implementing the next suggestion, and so on.

The truth is probably that your community is no closer to achieving community consciousness right now then it was several days ago when you picked up this book. What is closer though, is a complete understanding of the big picture and all the changes that need to be implemented in order to create community. If—and it is a very important 'if'—leadership understands, adopts and implements those changes and uses the tools of creating community, the gap between what "is" and what "can be" will eventually be so small that it will not even be noticeable. Trust in the transformative element of empowerment and its ability to create community.

CONCLUSION

The Beauty of Creating Community

Leadership is not so much about technique and methods as it is about opening the heart. Leadership is about inspiration—of oneself and of others. Great leadership is about human experiences, not processes. Leadership is not a formula or a program, it is a human activity that comes from the heart and considers the hearts of others. It is an attitude, not a routine. More than anything else today, followers believe they are part of a system, a process that lacks heart. If there is one thing a leader can do to connect with followers at a human, or better still a spiritual level, it is to become engaged with them fully, to share experiences and emotions, and to set aside the processes of leadership we have learned by rote.

Lance Secretan, Industry Week Magazine

Creating community is a beautiful process. It is beautiful, not in the sense that our culture defines it, but beautiful in its truest and most sublime form. These days glamorous is confused with beautiful. Movie stars, celebrities, homes, buildings, clothes are all glamorous. Make-up, the kind of car you drive, how you wear your hair, are the defining elements of being glamorous. Glamorous is what we are brainwashed by advertisers to believe is beautiful, but there is a big difference between glamour and beauty. We see an attractive man or woman in public or on the television and immediately label them a 'beautiful person.' However, that kind of 'beauty' is only skin deep, as they say.

True beauty is an experience of depth, awareness and form that elevates whoever beholds it beyond their current state of consciousness. When they say that beauty is in the eye of the beholder it is more a comment on the state of the beholder than it is of beauty. If one is able to see into the depths of a person or thing, understand its meaning, then beauty is certainly readily visible.

True beauty expands one's life and is something that many of us do not appreciate or embrace as much as we should these days. We sell-out what is genuine for what is convenient and easy to identify. You can buy the latest eyeliner from Cover Girl in order to become more glamorous and make one more attractive to the senses, but in order to become truly beautiful your character must evoke a pleasure that exalts the mind or spirit.

Creating community is a beautiful process. It brings out our most primitive nature to belong. It reinforces the inner satisfaction that knowing you are contributing to a cause that is greater than just yourself. It is the result of empowering a group of unique individuals and uniting them in the pursuit of common goals. Creating community expands one's life and makes us aware of our connection with those around us in ways that few life experiences can provide. Whether the community we are creating is within our neighborhood, our work environment, our social network, our city, our country or our world, the process of uniting others through empowerment is truly sublime and life altering.

As you set down this book and begin to reflect on its message and how you can begin to implement some of the ideas about creating community that have been presented, remember that you will need to start at the first step: yourself. When you understand how important your attitude is in order to facilitate community consciousness in others, you will naturally create the possibility of community all around you. Like the beacon of a lighthouse that shines out over a foggy sea, those people who you are working to empower and unite will see your actions through their own fog of disinterest, and begin to move towards your work. You can remain stuck in the fact that the members of your community just don't care or are unwilling to get involved. Or, you can recognize the possibility and potential of leading them into an awareness of community that will shift their focus and encourage choices of involvement. The first step is up to you.

If I could summarize, in one word, the essence of all of the teachings that I have tried to share with you in this book about creating community, you might be surprised at what that word is. We have talked about a great many things: uniting, communication, leadership, cooperation, empowerment, to name a few. But, as I have done throughout, I have to borrow the wisdom of another to explain what I believe lies at the deepest core of community. Towards the end of his life, Aldous Huxley was asked what he felt he had learned in his long, scholarly life journey. He answered, "I think just to be a bit kinder." Perhaps that is it . . . kindness.

REFERENCES

'*Introduction*
Dew, Dr. John Robert, Are You A Right-Brain or Left-Brain Thinker?, Quality Progress Magazine, April 1996, pp. 91-93.

Ned Hermann, Participant Memo (Los Angles, CA: The Whole Brain Corporation, 1982).

Brain Mind Bulletin, a publication of The Whole Brain Corporation in Los Angles, CA, Vol.6, No. 4 Aug. 24, 1981.

The Soul of Empowerment
Chodron, Pema: The Pema Chodron Collection; One Spirit, New York—pg 18-19.

Denver Post; November 27, 2006

Denver Post, November 28, 2006

Tao Te Ching, XXXIII

Simpkins, C. Alexander & Annellen: Simple Confucianism—A Guide to Living Virtuously; Tuttle Publishing, Boston—pg 89, pg 91, pg 93.

The Face of Empowerment
Hawkins, David R.; Power vs Force, Veritas Publishing, West Sedona, AZ 1995

Heider, John; The Tao of Leadership—Leadership Strategies for a New Age, Bantom Books, New York; pg. 59.

Kalekin-Fishman, D. (1996) 'Tracing the growth of alienation: Enculturation socialization, and schooling in a democracy', in Geyer, F. (ed.) *Alienation, Ethnicity, and Post-modernism*, London: Greenwood Press.

http://www.facebook.com/press/info.php?statistics, February 19, 2011

Ferrucci, Piero; The Power of Kindness, Penguin, New York; pg. 52.

Peck, M. Scott. (1987). *The Different Drum: Community Making and Peace*. Simon & Shuster.

Tuckman, Bruce (1965). "Developmental sequence in small groups". *Psychological Bulletin* 63 (6): 384-99

Cutler, Howard & His Holiness the Dalai Lama; The Art of Happiness (1998), Riverhead Books, New York: pg. 87.

http://www.vincelombardi.com/quotes.html, 2010

Cutler, Howard & His Holiness the Dalai Lama; The Art of Happiness (1998), Riverhead Books, New York: pg. 89.

Ciaramicoli, Arthur & Ketcham, Katherine (2000). "The Power of Empathy" Penguin Books, England. Pg. 158

Ferrucci, Piero; The Power of Kindness, Penguin, New York; pg. 16.

Shah, A. Tales of Afghanistan, London: Octagon, 1982

http://parentalwisdom.wordpress.com/2009/12/19/the-chinese-bamboo-story%E2%80%93-a-lesson-in-patience/, 2010

The Healing Power of Peer Pressure. Newsweek by <u>Abraham Verghese</u> March 06, 2011

Rosenberg, Tina, 2011; Join The Club, New York. W.W. Norton

Rosen, Mark J. Thank You for Being Such A Pain, New York: Three Rivers Press, 1998, pg. 57.

The Voice of Empowerment
Barnes, Jonathan, New England Condominium, May 2009, Farmington, MA,

Bradshaw, John, 1988, Healing The Shame That Binds You, Health Communications, Inc., Florida

Common Ground Magazine, July/August 1995, Community Associations Institute

A Course In Miracles, 1992; Foundation For Inner Peace, Mill Valley, CA

Pierson, Michael R., Taking Control—Time Management and Communication Tools for Community Association Management, 2006. Community Association Publishing Services, Palm Desert, CA

The Legs of Empowerment
Forming a Committee From The Board of Directors; Wiley Publishing, Indiana, March 2011

Keefe, Phillip, Form a Committee without Pain, June 2010, Suite101. com Media Inc.,Vancouver, B.C.

Roles of the Committee Chair, 2000; National Academy of Sciences, Washington, D.C.

Bly, Robert, *News of the Universe: Poems of Twofold Consciousness,* Sierra Books (San Francisco, CA), 1980.

The Heart of Empowerment
Brach, Tara, Ph.D, 2003, Radical Acceptance, Bantam Books, New York, pp. 283-284

Hanh, Thich Nhat, 2001, Anger—Wisdom for Cooling the Flames, Riverhead Books, New York, pg. 23

Holy Bible, King James Version, Genesis, Chapter 3, Verse 9, 10, 11, 12 & 13.

Campbell, Joseph, 1988, The Power of Myth with Bill Moyers, Broadway Books, New York

Boorstein, Sylvia, 2002, Pay Attention For Goodness' Sake, Ballantine Books, New York, pg. 272.

The Intelligence of Empowerment
Lozoff, Bo, 2000; It's A Meaningful Life—It Just Takes Practice, Viking Arkana, New York

Jaeckel LLC, 2007, www.LifeTrainingOnline.com—March 26, 2011.
Shed, Mark, http://www.leadership501.com/five-most-important-leadership-traits/27/

Freire, Paulo. *Pedagogy of the Oppressed.* New York: Continuum, 1982.

Knowles, M. S. (1980). *The modern practice of adult education: From pedagogy to andragogy.* Englewood Cliffs: Prentice Hall/ Cambridge

Attachment and Empowerment
http://www.conferenceboard.ca/hcp/details/society/acceptance-of-diversity.aspx, March30, 2011.

John S. & James L. Knight Foundation, www.knightfoundation.org. http://www.soulofthecommunity.org/about, March 30, 2011.

ACKNOWLEDGMENTS

First of all, thank you to my wife, Deborah, for her support, encouragement and wise advice and edits of my manuscript. You make me want to be a better person every single day.

Thank you to all of my readers and old friends who took the time to consider my work and provide their comments, suggestions and recommendations. I know every word sent to me was thoughtful and I truly appreciate all of your help and the time you invested in assisting me: Ron Orr, R.T. Gaffney, Julie Adamen, Lawrence Mayles, Jan Lhotka, Steven Shuey, Dana Detray, Tim Canfield & Dave Schultz.

Finally, thank you to my daughters, Amanda & Kellie, for your unconditional love and presence in my life. It is my hope that your lives are always touched by being involved in caring, healthy and supportive communities.

This book is dedicated to the memory of my great friend and brother John "Jai" Bats. Your life was an example of creating community and you knew instinctively how to unite others. Thank you for being my friend. I miss you.